7 Truths That Will Strengthen Your Marriage

Cesar Castellanos D.

Cesar Castellanos D © 2003
Published by G12 Editores
editorial@mci12.com

ISBN 1-932285-09-1

Impreso en Colombia
Printed in Colombia

Index

Dedication

With much love for the most beautiful, most anointed, and best mother.

Introduction

Living married together for twenty five years, gives us the authority to share the truth that have become the foundation of our marriage.

CHAPTER ONE

The first truth

Marriage is a Blessing

CHAPTER TWO

The second truth

MARRIAGE IS A MIRACLE

The miracle of having you at my side
When I wake up each morning and see you at my side, my heart fills with rejoicing.

God reserved you for me
The time that I have shared with you has made me see that God created you for me.

You are an exemplary woman
My love, you are an inspiration for those women who have lived through struggles and deceptions in their marriage, women who think that their problems cannot be solved.

The miracle of romance
We have cared for and protected that delicate flower daily. Being romantic in a marriage is like the body breathing oxygen.

God was our greatest ally
God became our great ally, transforming impossible things into that which is possible, helping us maintain hope.

The blessing of sexuality
God, who never makes a mistake, made us with sexual impulses.

Words full of love
Words should transform the chaotic into something beautiful and pleasant. With each word that leaves your mouth, one can bring a blessing or a curse.

The power of caresses
Your caresses, Claudia, have been like a balm that has brought refreshment to our home. I am fascinated when you draw near to me and caress me. It is a very meaningful gesture to me because it shows me that we are going down a good road.

CHAPTER THREE

The third truth

I MARRIED THE RIGHT PERSON

God promised me: «She will be your companion»
Since the day I met you, I knew that the Lord had already set aside a destiny for us to share

Asking god for signs
Thank you, Lord, for confirming to me that she will by my wife.

You are sure of yourself
Something that I have always admired about you is that you have quite a determined faith. This faith has become one of the pillars of our marriage.

The adversary's schemes

It is important that the husband always finds milk and honey in his home so that he can enjoy the pleasantness that marriage is.

We trusted in each other

One of your most outstanding things in you, is that you are not jealous

Opposite personality types

If married couples would understand that personality types in the hands of God are a great blessing, they would make more of an effort to have communion with Him.

CHAPTER FOUR

The forth truth

I HAVE DECIDED TO MAKE YOU HAPPY

Learning to be kind to your partner

Many people think that being kind to your partner is a sign of weakness. That is so far from reality!

Do not allow the man to be «macho»

Even though I have always tried to be kind to you, there was a moment when my attitude was not very good.

Hurtful words

Sarcastic words, which are like daggers even when untrue, are sometimes spoken in marriage.

Burying the past

Anyone who has been offended should make a stop in the way and make the decision to forgive wholeheartedly, burying the past and proposing never to bring it up again.

Remove all bitterness from your heart

Forgiveness is a decision.

Forgiving yourself

Accusations and blame come from the same fountain: A demonic power that tries to make human beings feel miserable.

CHAPTER 5

The fifth truth

THE POWER OF COMMUNICATION

The happiness of good communication

The number one problem in the majority of homes is the lack of effective communication.

Watch out for confusion!

I believe that in some homes the husband thinks one thing but expresses another with his mouth, and the rest understand something different.

The power of words

The greatest offenses are usually committed in moments of anger or desperation.

I give thanks to the lord because he has always allowed us to cultivate good communication in our home, a constant dialogue that is always progressing.

Using words that edify

You are a wise woman, the great artisan of the home that the lord has allowed us to build. Beloved claudia, you have always avoided using words of complaint; you have only permitted the language of faith.

Your words motivate

I believe that you never imagined the effect that your words would have on my life.

Your words bring comfort

Your words are like that, creating confidence, nourishment, and support. It is so important to know how to speak words to those who are weary.

CHAPTER 6

The sixth truth

BUILDING A GENERATION FOR GOD

Learning to be a father

God had to help me be a father because i lacked the guidance of a natural one who would explain to me how to educate my daughters.

I feel like the luckiest father

God has adorned our home with four princesses.

Letter to Johis, Lorena, Manuela, Sarita and Eliemerson.

Planting the best in our children

We plant positive attitudes

We plant integrity

We plant spirituality

We plant discipline

We plant a correct image

More golden rules to educate our children

Do not despise others, Do not ignore them, Bless your children

CHAPTER 7

The seventh truth

We Decided to be Guided by the Spirit of God

Epilogue

Dedication

To my beloved wife, Claudia

With much love for the most beautiful, most anointed, and best mother.

May each word expressed in this book be recorded in the deepest part of your heart because true love cannot be one-sided but rather it must be reciprocated so that it fulfills its purpose. And what has made our love beautiful is that we both have worked to make it grow. Although I want to have the eloquence of the most erudite speakers in order to choose each word with exquisite oratory skills and express to you in a thousand ways how I feel about you, I can only appeal to the sincerity of my heart because I believe that this is not only the best way to communicate but the most eloquent.

Introduction

«Wisdom builds her house; she has hewn out its seven pillars» (Proverbs 9:1).

We recently celebrated twenty-five years of marriage and when we sat down to think about which years were the most difficult, we realized that since the first moment there has been a lot of empathy between us and that we learned to talk about things without raising our voices. We also established the standard of making decisions by mutual agreement. In addition, we also learned which one of us had to give in, and we put that knowledge into practice. God guided us regarding the education of our daughters, but above all in the most important thing: how to keep alive the flame of love, always.

Having lived twenty-five happy years of marriage gives us authority to share the truths that have become the foundation of our marriage. We want our experience to be a blessing and inspiration in your life and for your family.

Marriage is not the idea of a man but the idea of God. God created man with the capacity to love and be loved. That is why it is very normal to be attracted to the opposite sex: a man towards a woman and a woman towards a man. God gave Adam a suitable helper, a companion who would be his support, and He made them both into a true team.

God was pleased to make marriage an extension of His own nature:

«So God created man in his own image, in the image of God he created him; male and female he created them» (Genesis 1:27).

The bounty of communication, peace, abundance, and greatness of God was extended to the human race through the first couple. If those pre-ordained principles of God had been accepted, we humans would not have gone through so many difficulties such as pain, sickness, misery, sadness, and deception.

God had carefully prepared a place where that first couple could dwell with their offspring. The Lord took into account even the smallest details so that they could be eternally happy. There was only one detail in which God did not want to intervene: the will that He had given to mankind.

That would come to be the inheritance that He entrusted to them so that they would administrate it however seemed best to them.

We can affirm that the basic principle of marital happiness is subject to the obedience of the couple to the Word of God. Although the couple may not be experts in topics that they address in marital relations, finances, the education of children, etc., the beginning of wisdom is the fear of the Lord.

It is important to understand God's intent to redeem marriages and families and to restore them to His original plan. This is essential so that our understanding can adjust to the divine purpose in relation to how to live effectively within the relationships that God has ordained for the family.

We connect the identity of a spouse and their children to the family's last name, but the truth is that this only identifies them superficially. The family's identity has deeper roots. «Family» is a word that is rooted in God. He told Abraham: «And all the families of the earth will be blessed in you» (Genesis 12:3b). We could ask ourselves why God chose Abraham as the instrument of blessing to all the families of the world. Maybe the response is due to the name of this man, but at that time he was the only one called «father.» And the character of a father is the closest that there is to the heart of God. Whoever is a good father will also be a good spouse, a provider, a protector, a guide, and a friend to his children.

Said in other words: a good relationship between a couple brings honor to the man, dignifies the woman, and gives their children security.

My prayer is that each page of this book becomes a fountain of not only information but also of blessing for your life, that by recovering your confidence in God you understand that even when it seems out of reach you can enjoy a good marriage.

It is also important that you understand that even though the message is directed at my wife, it is also the voice of nourishment, direction and comfort of God for your life.

I encourage the women who trust in God that in spite of adversities the Lord is an expert in doing miracles, and the most interesting is that He wants to use your faith to achieve them.

To the men, I exhort you to be inspired, to vanquish fear or indifference, and to dare to praise your wives with short phrases.

CHAPTER ONE

First truth

OUR MARRIAGE IS A BLESSING

«He who finds a good wife finds what is good and receives favor from the Lord» (Proverbs 18:22).

Dear Claudia: the greatest challenge that anyone faces is to build his own home. To accomplish that, you first have to analyze whether you can really finish this job. A marriage can only be built between two people, and it requires them both to give themselves completely to the divine purpose of raising a generation for God.

I thank God for each of the columns that have supported our marriage. One of the most important is to understand that even though two people are quite different, it pleases God to unite them in His time so that they will be one. And thanks to Him, we both decided voluntarily to submit our home fully to the divine plan. Due to that decision, we have seen His protection and care in every moment of our lives, and together we have felt that atmosphere of glory that can always be sensed in home.

We are witnesses that the blessing of God is integral. During the whole time that we have been married, we have grown spiritually, and we have realized that it does not mean anything to have plenty of material things if one of the two partners does not develop spiritually. No earthly thing can fill the void of a marital frustration.

Claudia, I thank God for your life because you have always known your place as a spouse, the wife of a pastor. Inside of you, there was a burning volcano, full of desire to erupt for God, longing to use all of your talents and abilities, combining them with the anointing of God to spread the truth of the gospel. But you wisely thought that the best way to achieve that was to repress all of that fire and to limit yourself to your role as wife.

In spite of this, you knew that my greatest desire was to see you involved in the ministry so that both of us would always speak the same language. You were aware that I never tried to limit you in your ministerial role.

Then who was it? The system? The tradition? The circumstances? Behind everything there was an adverse spiritual force that opposed the idea that the woman would develop as a leader. That is why I persevered in prayer, asking God to awaken your spirit for the ministry. The Lord responded to my prayers, and now I enjoy watching the development of your ministerial life. Claudia, without worrying about the price, you poured out your life in order to enlarge God's work. In a very short time, you have succeeded in having thousands of women train themselves for the Lord's work—nothing less than 13,000 women's cell groups. That is simply a result of your commitment to the Lord. You spent a lot of time preparing yourself, but we have had to wait five years in order to see your ministry explode in blessing.

Whoever knows you has seen you as a daring and valiant woman—yet fragile and tender at the same time, as delicate as a flower.

CONJUGAL BLESSING

Claudia, my love, after the Lord, you are my greatest blessing. You have brought Him such happiness into my soul that when I am at your side it is as if the time stands still and we enter into an eternal state. God has given you such sweetness that all of your words carry a dynamic faith and are adorned with glorious hope. All of your attitudes encourage conquest, and your caresses are so refreshing that one forgets that there are problems in this world. You are the most marvelous and simple woman. Everyone who knows you say it, but to you it seems like they exaggerate. The truth is that they fall short because they don't know you well enough. But as I live with you, I can tell you that you are the perfect woman. Not even a single day of the ones that we have shared have you brought sadness into my life but rather you have become in the flesh what God thought the ideal wife should be. You are very beautiful, and God thought of even the finest details the day He created you. I feel like the luckiest man in the world because God gave me a woman doubly beautiful.

Your internal beauty makes you very different than any other woman. No woman, however beautiful she may seem, will ever be equal to you.

OUR ENCOUNTER

Before knowing you, I was thinking a lot about what the companion that God would have for me would be like. I had so many ideas passing through my mind that it became impossible for me to imagine what the ideal woman would be like.

Then I gave up and said to the Lord:

«God, you see the future as well as the present and you designed beforehand the woman who is going to be my companion. I ask you in your mercy to bring her to me as soon as possible because if I choose I will make a mistake; therefore, please give her to me soon.»

And when I saw you for the first time, my heart began to beat so fast that it seemed that it was going to leave me. I did not know if it was a temptation or if it was my greatest blessing. Then I did the only thing that I could do: I took refuge in prayer. I quickly found a room where I could pray and when I presented this concern to the Lord, I felt that the whole room became illuminated, and I heard the voice of God, almost audibly telling me:

«My son, she will be your wife.»

Since I received that revelation, I have loved you with all my strength, and I began to guard your life in prayer. We did not know each other very well yet, and you were still totally unaware of what I had lived with the Lord. But that meeting also left a footprint in your life, and although we did not see each other again until several months later, the Lord had placed the seed of love in your heart.

Many people complain about marriage, but you have made the difference. You had many admirers, but your faith in the Lord was so great that you chose me. God will never take away the inheritance that He gave us. If you had looked at the circumstances, maybe I would not have qualified to be your husband. But your act of faith made me commit to the Lord to never defraud you.

MARRIAGE WAS GOD'S IDEA

Dear Claudia: The idea of marriage came from God. It is true that the first human being created was the man but even living in the midst of such beauty, he felt completely disoriented because he did not have anyone on his own level. Then God said, «It is not good for the man to be alone. I will make a helper suitable for him» (Genesis 2:18). God's idea to give him a companion was to make things simpler for him. God made the woman from the same nature as the man. Later, He brought her to him and blessed them.

Marital problems are due to countless mistakes that partners make when they choose a spouse. But God, in His great mercy, helps us to fix those mistakes and restore relationships; and He gives couples a second chance. Remember that for God, there is no such thing as a problem without a solution.

MARRIAGE IS AN ACT OF FAITH

Marriage is an act of faith in every aspect because people decide to coexist with someone who they may not even have known existed a few years earlier. But mutual attraction leads to love, and that love carried them to make the decision to unite their lives according to the laws of their respective countries, but also before God, whom they have never seen yet know to be real, and that He will establish His peace and blessing within the family and its descendants.

You and I have always liked working with marriages, and we have seen thousands of homes restored by divine grace. None of the couples that work with us in the ministry, including thousands of lay leaders, have gone through divorce. This has helped us to enrich the ministry, and when marriages are strengthened, the nation becomes greater.

PHYSICAL BLESSING

«I praise you because I am fearfully and wonderfully made; your works are wonderful, I know that full well» (Psalm 139:14).

The beauty of wisdom has been poured out on you. My love: you are unique. To see you is to know divine wisdom. Each detail

I remember a conversation that I had with a friend who was going through many marital problems. Before my question, «How do you treat your wife?» he affirmed, «I like to receive affection, but it costs me a lot to give it.» Then I realized that the root of this man' marital problems were burried in his childhood because his parents were not at his side when he needed them most. This situation left in him a great emotional void that nothing had been able to fill. I made him see that God is our true Father, and that if his human parents have failed him, his heavenly Father was very real and was at his side in order to fill every void in his life. While I was explaining this to him, he was moved. We agreed in prayer, and he poured out his heart, saying, «Dad, where were you when I needed you most? Why did you leave when I depended on you the most? But dad, I forgive you, I bless you, and I love you.» After that prayer, he got up and told me, «I believe I have a debt with my wife and my children. I am going to ask forgiveness for all of the love that I have denied them. I could not be authentic because I had a completely distorted image of myself, and therefore I denied my family happiness.»

EVERY PERSON IS UNIQUE

Each person is unique in this world. Although they calculate that the population of the earth is about six billion, the interesting thing is that it is not possible to meet two people that are the same. Each one is unique. Many human beings have suffered every kind of emotional distress, and they have been wounded by those whom they love the most. The enemy has tried to destroy the self-image given by God, but the Lord prepared a plan to restore the identity of each person. That is why he offers us an invitation that says, «'Return to me,' declares the Lord Almighty, 'and I will return to you'» (Zechariah 1:3b). That is the promise established by God—if someone becomes one with Him, He will do the same with that person.

THE TOUCH OF THE MASTER

Do you remember that story that I have shared in some of my talks? I am referring to the story about the old violin that was offered for twenty dollars in a public auction. No one was giving more because it was an ugly, old, faded violin. When the sale was about to close because no one was showing any interest in it, someone burst into the auditorium, went to the front, picked up the violin, tuned it, and began to play. The sound was so extraordinary and beautiful that the atmosphere of the auditorium changed, and the people stopped worrying about the outer appearance of the violin and began to appreciate the quality of its sound. The instrument sold at an excellent price.

What made the big difference was something that we could call «the touch of the master.» The deepest wounds that a human being has suffered have been caused by the people closest to him. Whoever says that he loves us is also accustomed to hurting us, and this makes us feel like an old, useless violin. but if we let Jesus, the master of excellence, touch us, He will fill us so that each of us recovers our own identity. He is the only one who can fully heal hearts or souls that have been broken into pieces. There is nothing more to do than to let him pour His oil and His wine on us to heal our wounds. If we do this, we will feel that Jesus is more real than any person that we can touch because although we do not see him with our physical eyes, the effects of his healing touch leave the fragrance of His presence. He wants us to enjoy His emotional blessing. Each person should appropriate the passage that says:

«Praise be to the God and Father of our Lord Jesus Christ, who has blessed us in the heavenly realms with every spiritual blessing in Christ» (Ephesians 1:3)

CHAPTER TWO

Second truth

MARRIAGE IS A MIRACLE

THE MIRACLE OF HAVING YOU AT MY SIDE

When I wake up each morning and see you at my side, my heart fills with rejoicing and my lips give thanks to God for the miraculous way that He united us. He caused us to meet. If it had not been for Him we would never have seen how close we were. I know nothing was a coincidence; everything that happened after our first time we met was directed by the hand of God.

ENDURING TRIALS

One of the strongest tests of my Christian life occurred right after I got saved. I had been going to a small church for about six months. Because I was the only Christian in my house, my family did not understand my new life, and I had to live outside of my house for a year. The most appropriate place that I found was that small church, but I never imagined the tests that I would have to face in that place. I shared my room with the son of a lady who said she was a pastor, but her attitudes as well as her actions said exactly the opposite. After living in that place for a few days, a young girl arrived at the house, and she was given accommodations in another room. This girl and the pastor made an agreement to convince me to have a sentimental relationship with the girl. My only interest was to grow in the Lord, so a relationship with the girl was not important to me. The woman who called herself a pastor appealed to prophecy. I was a newborn Christian and was not able to fully discern it. According to the prophecy that the woman gave me, that girl would definitely be my wife. And so with that, the groundwork was done to achieve what those two wanted.

One morning, my roommate left very early for work. Then the girl immediately entered my room and lay down beside me. When I woke up and saw her, I asked her why she was in my bed. She said, «Since I am going to be your wife, I want you to treat me as such from today on.» This was a moment of great struggle in my mind, with the supposed prophecy in between, the insinuation of the girl, and the desires of the flesh. But in the midst of the test, a thought came to me that I could recognize as coming from the Spirit of God: «Supposing that she becomes your wife, you should not be intimate with her until you are married.» That thought gave me the strength to ask her to leave the room.

Since that moment, I intensified my level of prayer until I understood that I had to leave that place. God gave me wisdom to do it without hurting anyone. I had the full certainty that the strength of a ministry depended in great measure on the person that one chooses as a marriage partner because this person can lift us up or bury us. For that reason, I put the whole matter in God's hands.

On the same day God showed me in three different passages of His Word what a false prophecy is. Immediately, I jumped with joy saying, «Lord, thank you for not letting it be that girl.» The truth is that I did not feel anything for her at all.

Later, God gave me strength to confront those two women and to tell them that I was not in agreement with that prophecy. Imagine the look of astonishment and disgust on the face of the woman who claimed to be a pastor. What she did then was to change her strategy to try to break me in another way. Kindly she told me: «Cesar, if you do not take this woman that God has given you, you will have to remain like Paul because you lost the only opportunity that God had for you. That is why I suggest that you take the vow of celibacy.» And right at that moment she bombarded me with her insistent and only question: «Did you take the vow yet? Remember you will not be able to marry anyone because you chose the path of a single man when you rejected the woman that God had for you.»

The pressure was so strong that I felt as if this woman was brainwashing me. One afternoon in the middle of prayer, I felt tempted to take the famous vow, but a voice inside me delayed me saying, «Don't do it.» That same night I had a dream. God spoke to me prophetically: «Young man, do not be afraid because

I have a companion for you.» Later the Lord told me that I would leave that place because there was nothing there for me to do.

My love, God guarded me from the claws of that fierce woman. Later, I found out that that girl had a spirit of prostitution. Regarding that woman who claimed to be a pastor, she and her house have been in complete misery.

Although the adversary does not know the future, he can detect people who have a call to ministry and tries to trap them any way possible to put him as far as possible from the divine plan. I believe that if I had fallen into that trap of the enemy my life would have been totally different to what it is now, including family and ministry. But I give thanks to God for having guarded me for you and also for having reserved you for me. You are the exact opposite of that woman; you are sweetness, goodness, love, prudence, and holiness. The adversary wanted to interfere in our encounter, but the purpose of God prevailed.

GOD RESERVED YOU FOR ME

When I read in Genesis that God formed the woman from the man's rib and that He later presented her to him, I understood that you are part of my same nature. The time that I have shared with you has made me see that all that the Bible says is exact: God created the woman for the man. This means that while God was working in my life in one way, He was also working in your life in another way. That is why when we met both of knew that we were made one for the other.

After so many years of sharing everything, I know that life would not have made sense if you were not at my side. Of all the miracles that I have received, I can say that after salvation, you are the most pleasant.

When I was a single man, feeding uncertainties regarding my future wife, I believe that the heavenly Father commissioned the Holy Spirit to look for the right spouse for me, so she would fight shoulder to shoulder with me.

When Abraham's servant met Rebekah and saw her spirit of service in addition to being very beautiful and of the same family of his master Abraham, he bowed down and worshipped God because he knew that she was the one God was showing him to be Isaac's wife. Then he overwhelmed the girl and her family with jewels and gifts. The Holy Spirit has done the same with you. He saw that you had a servant's heart, that you were a woman inclined towards the things of God, as well as being beautiful. When I saw you I said: «Father, I have found her.» Then He filled you with the most precious jewels. In all that you are, the gifts of the Spirit of God can be detected in your life. Just as He did with Rebekah, God also has blessed you. The Holy Spirit was the great ally in our meeting and in our relationship. For that reason, I bless Him continuously because I truly love you.

YOU WERE CHOSEN AND PROTECTED BY GOD

Just as God gave the woman to the first man, He brought you to me in His time. I am completely sure that our marriage was planned in heaven and that the angels of God guarded our lives from every emotional mislead.

After God freed me from that test in the house of that pastor, I met a young girl who was very attractive and I was excited about her. I did not know her very well, but I liked her. At that time, I really enjoyed going to the mountains to pray. One day, after spending quite a while in that place, I got hungry. In my country there is a very tasteful fruit called guayaba. Close to me there was a guayaba tree, and it occurred to me to take one of the fruits. They were too high up to reach, however, so I took some stones to try to knock one down. No matter how many stones I threw, however, I could not knock that guayaba down.

Later, I focused on another guayaba that was much higher and told myself, «I am going to try that one.» Imagine my surprise when the fruit fell after I threw the first stone. When I picked it up, I saw that it was a large fruit that was very ripe. When I went to taste it, I heard the voice of the Spirit tell me, «Son, do not insist any more on that girl; she is like that guayaba that did not fall. No matter how much you say it to her, she is not going to be for you. Each attempt to win her was like one of the stones that you threw at the first guayaba. The companion that I have for you is in a higher place. Just like the fruit that you knocked down, she is completely mature, balanced in every way—physically, spiritually, emotionally, and intellectually.»

Then I knew that the miracle had already happened. God had worked in your life through your parents. He was guarding your emotions and feelings. He protected you from unpleasant experiences. He cared for you so that you would not open your heart to the wrong person. Although some people tried to win your heart, attracted by your beauty, you always were very firm in your decisions. Thanks to that, God protected you so that you would not get hurt. That is why when I saw you for the first time I heard the voice of the Spirit tell me, «She is the woman that I compared to that ripe guayaba. You are near the woman that is going to be your wife.»

God was preparing our encounter, which was surprising and marvelous. Just as Isaac loved Rebekah from the moment that he saw her, the same thing happened to me. There has not been a single day in our marriage when I have not enjoyed loving you. Every day I feel the need to tell you that I love you, and although you already know it, I have to repeat it time after time. If I cannot tell you verbally, I send you a note: «Claudia, do not forget that I love you.»

YOU ARE AN EXEMPLARY WOMAN

My love, you are an inspiration for those women who have lived through struggles and deceptions in their marriage, women who think that their problems cannot be solved. Each word that leaves your mouth has given light and hope to many of these women. I even remember the case of that lady who came up to you looking for advice despite feeling very «dirty» for having been unfaithful to her husband. Then you told her the story of that young girl who stained her new dress with ink at her fifteenth birthday party. When her mother saw her crying and thought that her party was ruined, she took the dress and skillfully made a pretty accessory of the same color as the stain and enhanced the beauty of the dress even more. You made that unfaithful woman see that God does the same with our mistakes. All of our failures are transformed into blessings in His hands. After you prayed for her, that woman felt like a new woman with all the strength that she needed in order to grow in God.

THE MIRACLE OF ROMANCE

Remember that time shortly after we met when I had an accident and I was recovering in my house? You came to see me and brought me some fruit in your bag, but you did not dare to give them to me. I know that you wanted to show me your love, but you did not do it, perhaps due to the circumstances or the other people who were there?

Romance is like that: we bring everything very carefully, but it costs a lot to take it out of the bag. Today, we laugh when we remember that episode, and we ask ourselves, «Why is it so difficult for human beings to express their feelings?»

Some people do it and do not receive the response that they deserve. Then they become inhibited and are not the least bit interested in trying to do it again. But this response is not healthy; we all have to learn to conquer fear, to move in faith, and to try again.

At first, we did not know how to be romantic, and so we made a lot of mistakes. I remember the first time that I asked you to go out with me. I ignored the fact that the romantic part of a woman is stimulated by words of flattery and appreciation, by everything that makes her feel like the only one in the universe. We had walked who knows how many blocks when I took your hand, pulled you close to me, and kissed you. I even remember the expression of shock on your face. Your eyes pierced me and you said, «What happened to you? What you are doing is not romantic for a woman.» I thought that such actions were the only way to express love.

It is incredible that God would make us so different in order to unite us later and make us understand that we are the perfect complements for each other: you, so shy and reserved and me, so extroverted and impulsive. Something that surprised me in a big way is that the flame of that romantic love never has diminished in our marriage. We have cared for and protected that delicate flower daily. Being romantic in a marriage is like the body breathing oxygen. You need my words; I need your caresses. You need my caresses; I need your words.

What elevates the quality and category of a hotel is the attention to details. Marriages work the same way: what improves a home is something small, at the level of a detail. Many people do not understand that and think that romance begins at ten or eleven o'clock at night, after a hard day's work. They go straight to the point, thinking that they fulfill their conjugal duty that way, but we know that conjugal intimacy is the culmination of a series of small and pleasant details that have been produced throughout the whole day. If there are moments of hostility and aggression in a home, the atmosphere is absolutely not conducive to intimacy. Those are the moments when many people—almost always women—feel humiliated and abused.

A man told me, «It is becoming very difficult for me to tell my wife that I love her. Each time that I try to do it, I get a lump in my throat and the words do not come out.»

I told him, «If you do not flatter your wife, another man will do it for you.» Our Lord tells us that the husband should praise his wife (Proverbs 31:28b).

Romance is like a thermometer: when the marriage goes well, the romantic love is stable; when something goes bad, it freezes. We should never allow difficulties to rob us of the miracle of romantic love.

THE MIRACLE OF LOVE

Since the first moment that I saw you, I experienced a series of diverse feelings. I almost stopped breathing. My heart began to beat faster. I felt cold, hot, nervous, amused. I wanted to make the best impression on you. That day I was sure that the woman of my dreams was standing before me: sweet, tender, sure of herself. Everything that you did, every word that you spoke, every gesture that you made was precious and firm like the melody of an excellent orchestra or a parade of cavalry.

But the most important thing was still missing: God's approval. That is why I sought it in prayer, deciding to accept you if this encounter came from His Spirit and to reject it in the name of Jesus if it was a product of temptation. That same instant I heard the voice of God: «Son, do not be afraid; she will be your wife.» I felt like a general who wins his greatest battle, like a diver who searches for pearls and finds the most beautiful one.

That day, I threw myself face down and worshiped the Lord with my whole heart. I rested in Him, waiting for His time to culminate the miracle. The way we met was something more than a mere physical or sexual attraction because you were the other half of my life, and I had finally found you.

GOD WAS OUR GREATEST ALLY

Other days and weeks and months of persevering in prayer followed that day. I was begging God to continue working in us, but the most interesting thing of all was that He was already involved in the matter. He became our great ally, transforming impossible things into that which is possible, helping us maintain hope.

When I was sure that you were the woman chosen by God for me, I decided to walk in faith. I behaved as if I was already married. When I went home in the afternoon, I had the feeling that my beautiful wife would be awaiting my arrival. In my mind, I imagined us complementing each other in the ministry. I felt like the luckiest man in the world. Today, after looking back, I realize that I have lived out everything I dreamed and even more with you.

Claudia, I know that I love you because you are part of me, that part that was missing. I thank God that He kept me for you and you for me because I do not feel the weight of the things of life with you beside me. You know how to confront difficulties in a very special way because God has given you the ability to convert difficult things into simple things. You only see the biggest adversity in a positive way; you always see the good in difficult people. That is why I dare to say that you have learned to see things with the eyes of God. Claudia, thanks for having believed in me and for allowing us to build a generation for God together.

LOVE AT FIRST SIGHT

Each time that I read the story of Isaac and Rebekah, the incredible supernatural way that those young people met, I identify completely with the story. I know that when the Holy Spirit bore witness to your spirit regarding us, you believed Him just like Rebekah. And by this act of faith, you also believed my words, even though you did not know me. And just as Eliezer gave beautiful and expensive gifts to Rebekah, the Spirit gave you the best and most beautiful gifts for your act of faith. And just as Isaac loved Rebekah as soon as he saw her, I loved you from the first moment. I loved you, and I have never stopped loving you. Genesis 24 teaches us that Isaac and Rebekah loved each other for several reasons:

1. *Both were directed by God.*
2. *The Holy Spirit was in charge of the meeting.*
3. *They both knew to wait on God.*
4. *They both renounced their own interests.*
5. *They both decided to serve God, which is why they were prospered.*

UNDERSTANDING THE LANGUAGE OF LOVE

Love is the most powerful force in the universe; it is what motivates us to make the most difficult decisions, to climb the highest mountains, to conquer the most feared armies, and to break the thickest chains.

From the moment that a creature is conceived in the womb of the mother and throughout its development—birth, growth, and formation—it receives expressions of love directly from God or expressed through others.

But it is one thing to receive and to feel love and another thing altogether to express it. People who have not been able to express love are unable to do so because they believe that they have not received it. But whether we believe it or not, love has been offered to every human being because we are all expressions of God's love. Those to whom love is revealed are quite fortunate because it is the force that sustains the universe, the power that has preserved humanity through all time, the hymn that creation interprets each day. Human words, however eloquent they may be, do not even touch the shoreline of the ocean of love. People who have succeeded in binding their spirit to the spirit of love are the only ones who can understand it. Only those who never have changing attitudes. Only those who do not let themselves become confused by the indifference of others. Love is the only thing that exists by itself. Before the eyes, the heart of man is naked. His love was so great that He gave what was most wanted to rescue many.

THE EXPRESSION OF LOVE IS TO GIVE

To many people, it becomes difficult to express love when they get to the point where it is their turn to give. They make the mistake of getting used to receiving and deprive themselves of the privilege of giving. A genuine relationship is one where each partner gives to the other, fighting for each other's well being and the well being of the marriage. A genuine gift goes beyond the physical relationship. True love offers not only the body but it also commits its feelings. The one who is inclined to give everything will receive an overabundance of blessing in return. Abraham illustrated this idea. He was inclined to sacrifice his own son to show His love for God.

Paul eloquently directs the men of Ephesus, insisting that they love their wives as Christ loved His church, with each man laying down his life for his wife (Ephesians 5:25). Later, John reprimands this same church for having lost the first love, romantic love. (Revelations 2:4).

GESTURES

Your look has taught me that I am not always right in everything that I do and say, as I used to think before. When I saw that expression on your face, showing me my error without words, it was disconcerting, and I thought that obeying you would be symptomatic of having little manhood. What a mistaken idea. By the mercy of God, however, I decided to set aside my pride and understand your language. That decision brought a lot of stability to our marriage. I realized that you have what some people call a sixth sense. Feminine intuition, others say, or spiritual discernment. Whatever it is, is a precious gift that the Lord has only given to women. And today I know that this is simply to see the circumstances through my other two eyes. You see more than my eyes. To understand this has helped us to work better as a team. Now I am able to read all of your expressions and discern your thoughts. We have come to the place where we complement each other completely; we are each one for the other.

THE BLESSING OF SEXUALITY

God, who never makes a mistake, made us with sexual impulses. Did He do that in order to torment us? Obviously not. In His Word, He established the parameters so that conjugal intimacy reaches its full development, placing blessing and not guilt. The bible tells us that the men of God were holy and had healthy marriages, enjoying perfect relationships with their spouses.

God approves sexual love only in a married couple. That is why we discourage young people from experimenting with that which is reserved for marriage. When the sexual experience develops within this framework, with a healthy mind, without malice, the mutual confidence of the couple grows a lot, as does their peace, respect, security, and love.

I have come to the conclusion that intimate problems of almost every couple have to do with the area of the mind because that is where the biggest walls of distancing arise that lead marriages down the path of confusion, frustration, or separation. Sadly, the information about sexuality which the majority of teenagers receive is neither correct nor appropriate because the channels through which the communication flows have been touched by evil. As a result, many young people and adolescents throw themselves into this fascinating and dangerous new world to explore it. Some stay trapped in their past and suffer the consequences of their own curiosity.

On the other hand, some religious extremists have come to believe that sexual intimacy with your partner reduces your spiritual strength and makes you lose a certain degree of holiness, to the point that sexual intimacy with their husband or wife fills them with guilt.

Adam and Eve were naked but they were not ashamed. There was transparency and innocence. It is so important that each couple recovers that lost innocence. This is possible if the relationship with the Holy Spirit is restored through the Word that helps us renew our minds and carries us to the genuine and true fountain.

The Word of God cleans us and shows us the true meaning of sexuality. God created the man with sexual impulses so that the couple becomes a permanent fountain of re-creation and so that everything will not be monotony and work. The problems come when the laws of marriage are broken and one of the partners throws himself or herself into extramarital adventures. Solomon said that whoever does that will be hurt and ashamed and the insult will never be erased. But he also said, «May your fountain be blessed, and may you rejoice in the wife of your youth, a loving doe, a graceful deer—may her breasts satisfy you always, may you ever be captivated by her love» (Proverbs 5:18-19).

I have loved you every day of our twenty-five years of marriage. You have been that beloved servant, and you have filled my life with happiness because you have understood me in all areas. Your caresses have been like a fresh breeze and have affected every particle of my being. With your affectionate gestures, you have written the most beautiful love poem, a poem that only I can read because it is carved into the deepest part of my heart.

It is incredible that sexuality for some people is only the pleasure of the moment. Conjugal intimacy should be the culmination of words of encouragement, respect, and affection that the couple transmits throughout the day or the week. No one wants to feel treated like an object; that is why sexuality cannot be separated from the harmony that should exist inside the life of a couple. Just like a good wine, romantic love should get better with age.

WORDS FULL OF LOVE

Words should transform the chaotic into something beautiful and pleasant. With each word that leaves your mouth, one can bring a blessing or a curse because words are weighted with a power that activates the angelic realm or the powers of darkness. This is even true when you are joking.

A while ago, we had a couple of missionaries staying in our home. One morning, Claudia, I greeted you the way I always did at that time: «Hi, little fat one. How are you?»

«The shocked missionary's wife asked me, «What did you call her?»

«Little fat one,» I responded.

«Why do you call her that?» she asked.

«It's a term of affection here in our country» I said.

«That is not a term of affection for a woman,» she replied. «There are other words that sound much better. You can call her 'Perfect one.'»

How ignorant we were of the power of words! I suppose that no one, however fat he or she may be, likes to be referred to that way. I believe the missionary's wife was definitely right and calling you «Perfect one» has served well because even though the years pass, it is unnoticeable in you.

THE POWER OF CARESSES

When Isaac caressed his wife, the king Abimelech realized that she was his wife and not his sister as they had pretended. Caresses are revealing. They are the thermometer of the heart.

Your caresses, Claudia, have been like a balm that has brought refreshment to our home. I am fascinated when you draw near to me and caress me. It is a very meaningful gesture to me because it shows me that we are going down a good road. It is like when a coach gives a pat on the back of an athlete to let him know that he is doing very well. If there are no caresses in a home, the stimulation to continue forward is lacking, monotony is hurried into the relationship.

To wait for a caress that does not come is like taking the salary away from a worker, like unfairly punishing someone who did no wrong. Thanks to God, however, you are the most caring woman in the world, and I never get tired of your caresses. For my part, I always have been caring; it is something that is very rooted in my personality. What a delight that my caresses are returned.

CHAPTER THREE

Third truth

I MARRIED THE RIGHT PERSON

GOD PROMISED ME:
«She will be your companion»

Although I was sure of the destiny that the Lord had already drawn up for us since the day I met you, when I look at the circumstances that surrounded our relationship everything seemed to indicate that it was something unattainable. I had the promise but at the same time I saw you very far away from me. At that time, my only refuge was prayer: I began to ask the Lord for all kinds of confirmations.

I remember that a few months after we met while I was in prayer, I received a prophecy that shook my heart. The Spirit of God told me the following: «Son, I have chosen you so that you will serve me, and I will show myself through you, with signs and wonders. And the woman that is now beside you will be your companion and I will also manifest myself through her with miracles, sings and wonders» That day, I went out looking for you, I was excited and I told you what the Lord had revealed to me. I still remember the look of shock on your face. Your reaction was to tell me: «That cannot be; I believe that it is all just your own idea.» I responded, «I am completely sure that it is the voice of God because that is His way of speaking to me.»

ASKING GOD FOR SIGNS

A little while after that conversation, I went to the country one day. I was walking, thinking about what you had said to me. Then I asked the Lord to give me another sign, and while I was thinking about what kind of sign to ask for, I heard a child calling me, asking me to help with some sheep that had spread out.

Then the Lord told me, «Here is the sign that you asked me for. Go and count the sheep. If there are eight, this is the signs; if there are not eight, it is not.» Those words filled me with fear because I did not want to think about losing you. I ran quickly to where the sheep were, and I only counted five. Then I closed my eyes, thinking, «It can't be!» But when I opened my eyes I realized that two more had appeared, and the boy had another one, making it eight sheep in all. With all my heart I said, «Thank you, Lord, for confirming to me that she will by my wife.»

But two months later as I thought about all that had happened to us and the sign of the eight sheep, I told the Lord, «Father, it is not that I do not trust your promises, but I would like to ask you for one last confirmation—this time from your Word, that in the place where I open the bible on the left side in verse 8 you will confirm this relationship for me.» I opened the bible full of faith, knowing that my hands were directed by the Lord. I almost fainted when I read, «And the two will become one flesh; so they are no longer two but one» (Mark 10:8). After that I said, «Lord, I do not have anything more to add; take complete control of this relationship and bless my future wife.» Full of joy, I later saw how you were growing in faith, and I know that it was the Lord who changed the appearance of things so that our marriage would become a reality.

OTHERS WANTED TO DECIDE FOR US

When we left that little chapel where we got married, it seemed to me like a dream that had finally united our lives. Rumors were flying—some in favor of the marriage and some against us. One of your aunts went to the extreme of giving your mother condolences. «My daughter did not die,» was her wise response.

To a family so stuck in catholic tradition, it was almost impossible for them to imagine that you could have a future with someone committed to Christian principles. I know that that situation was very difficult for your parents because they had to endure comments that were not flattering. Your parents began to think that you had made a mistake, that our relationship would not last long and that very soon you would be returning home.

It was incredible to see how the people who surrounded us tried to decide for us. Maybe they thought that you were not mature enough to do it alone. They simply ignored that if anyone is directed by God, there is no risk of making a mistake like people who make impulsive decisions based on their own desires.

YOU ARE SURE OF YOURSELF

Something that I have always admired about you is that you have quite a determined faith. This faith has become one of the pillars of our marriage. And I ask God not to allow me to fail the woman who had the courage to marry me.

Although every home goes through tests and adversity, I have always been completely sure that I was the only man for you and that you are the only woman for me. I never questioned your youth. There are those who justify marital failures by the youth of their partners, but this never occurred in our case. On the contrary, it has been a very rich experience for us to grow together in all areas without having to go through the process of healing wounds that result from past mistakes.

Although some people are attracted by something concrete in the other person, everything about you drew my attention: your beauty, your heart, your sweetness, your maturity, your purity. There was absolutely nothing to change. And today, many years later, you continue to enjoy these same qualities with the added sweet touch of experience.

NEVER ALLOW THIRD-PARTY INTERFERENCE

It seems to me like if I was looking at you today: you were pregnant with our first daughter, and looked tender and delicate. At that time, we were living in my parents' house, but we always maintained our privacy because we had proposed that neither your relatives nor mine would interfere negatively in our marriage. So our home had very powerful walls of protection; we felt as if the Lord Himself was around our home like a powerful giant.

That day, I wanted to help you wash the clothes, and I was surprised to meet one of my sisters, who looked shocked as if I had done something wrong. She said to me, «Where are you going?»

Without giving much importance to her reaction I told her, «I want to help my wife wash these clothes.» By the expression on her face I realized that she did not agree with my decision. Later, she told me, «Isn't it better for her to go down and do it?»

I responded abruptly, «This is my home and I direct it however I think is best, so I ask you not to try to interfere with our relationship.» My sister thought that she was doing me a big favor, but if I listened to what she was telling me it could have provoked a confrontation.

THE ADVERSARY'S SCHEMES

We have always cared for our home as if it was the most sacred one in the world, but sometimes—for doing good to others—we have made mistakes. That was what happened when your heart was touched and you tried to help that young girl who had fought with her husband. We gave her a place to stay in our home with her two little children, but she tried to flirt with me. When we realized the mistake that we had made, we had to get her out of there immediately.

So many women have fallen into the trap of the enemy, letting those who pretend to be their best friends rob them of their husbands. We know that the best protection for marriages is to always guard the harmony as a couple and to remain very alert in the marriage in order not to give a strange woman or man a place. It is important that the husband always finds milk and honey in his home so that he can enjoy the pleasantness that marriage is.

WE TRUST ONE ANOTHER

One of your best qualities is that you are not jealous. Jealousy is a symptom of insecurity and distrust, and there have been many problems and injustices committed because of them. Jealous people torment not only themselves but everyone around them.

Do you remember that man who was consumed with jealousy who sought my counsel? He told me that when he got home he searched under the beds, in the closet, everywhere, because he was sure that his wife was unfaithful. One day, when he went to drive his vehicle, he suddenly saw his wife's car. Imagine his surprise to see her accompanied by another man. He tried to control himself and he began to follow them without them noticing. While they headed towards the outskirts of the city, every possible negative thought crossed his mind, and he said to himself, «This will be the end for both of them.» He hoped that they would pass by a certain place where there were several cliffs with the firm intention of finishing them. When he was at the point of crashing his car into theirs, already prepared to culminate his purpose and knock them into the depths of the abyss, he glanced at them one last time to say goodbye to his wife. He was quite surprised to realize that the woman was not his wife and the car was not her car. This whole incident was controlled by jealousy.

When this man finished sharing his experience, I made him see that jealousy is a demonic spirit that had entered his being because of his own insecurity towards his wife. I explained to him that he should renounce every doubt and form of distrust towards her and begin to fill his mind with images of faith and hope.

OPPOSITE PERSONALITY TYPES

My father-in-law's home is unique. «We are like water and oil,» was the expression that was always on their lips. You and I made them see that opposites attract, that one person has what the other lacks and that God made us with opposite temperaments to complete each other as a couple. Although it took them a while to accept this, now we can see how two people complement each other completely.

If married couples would understand that personality types in the hands of God are a great blessing, they would make more of an effort to have communion with Him. Although your temperament is quite docile and mine is quite strong, we have always succeeded in maintaining harmony. Although there have been no fights in our home, we did have some disagreements at the beginning. That was something that marked me forever in my relationship with you. We had had a difference, perhaps over some insignificant thing, so I addressed you with a strong tone of voice. That hurt you so much that you began to cry, and despite knowing that you were suffering, I did not think it was important and became indifferent. In that moment the Spirit of God spoke to my heart and said, «With this thing that you have done to your wife, you are hurting yourself. Don't you know that she is flesh of your flesh and bone of your bones? To hurt her is to detest yourself, as if your own hand struck your face.» When I received this divine revelation, I repented immediately and made the decision not to offend you ever again. And to this day, I have made the effort to fulfill that intent.

Although the bible teaches that the two will become one flesh, at times it is hard for us humans to make that a reality. With our experience helping so many married couples, we know that through most conflicts that arise, even those values that may have been lost can be restored. We see this in the faces of some of them that now are developing as leaders. Even the appearance of their faces has changed; they are very different to when we met them. They had the courage to believe God, and with His strength they overcame their own problems and passed to the other side. Not only this, but they have also become a blessing for thousands of families. This makes us think that there is indeed hope in God for all that He desires to save in the home.

CHAPTER FOUR

Fourth truth

I Have Decided to Make you Happy

To be married to you has filled me with happiness. During all these years of sharing our lives, not one day has brought sadness to my heart—not even the least. When I thought about the reasons that we enjoy such complete harmony, the Lord showed me that one of those factors is that since the day I met you I made the decision to try to make you the happiest woman in the world. Paul gave us a very practical lesson with respect to this: «A man reaps what he sows» (Galatians 6:7b). That love that I planted in you is something I have been able to harvest as well.

I believe that selfishness is the cause of many problems that affect families today. Unfortunately, many men enter marriage with the wrong idea that it is the woman who should make them happy. I hope we understand that happiness does not occur when we try to obtain it from others but rather when we offer it. God designed human beings so that they can receive and express love, it is a two way street.

Our deepest wounds in the emotional realm have been caused by whoever has claimed to love us. Many times, a person enters marriage with countless wounds from childhood that were caused by the lack of parents' affection, by rejection, or by not having been the preferred child. These acts leave profound marks on the heart—marks that time does not erase. Afterwards they get married believing that marriage is the way to forget all of that suffering. But the only thing that happens is that the wounds actually grow larger. Wounds to the spirit go beyond memory. They are so deep that many times our mind does not even see where they are.

CAUSES OF HAVING A WOUNDED SPIRIT

Through all these years of helping married couples, we have observed that the great majority of partners have lived through stormy conditions in their homes. The result is that their hearts are so full of wounds that some of them come to lose their identity.

Do you remember that woman who opened her heart to us and shared her story? When she got married, she thought she had found the most wonderful person in the world. She was impressed by all that her husband seemed to be: an honest person full of good principles and refined manners. A flood of likeable details won her heart. When they got married, she painted in her mind a picture full of illusions: her future. But that whole marvelous picture was destroyed the first night as a married woman. Her husband got angry over something insignificant, lost control, and hit her. That act foreshadowed what her marriage would be like: daily beatings for ten years. The words of contempt and the violence obscured the identity of that woman because she began to believe that she would never be worth anything by herself. The situation led her to divorce. Later, she could take refuge in God. Her heart was healed and her life was restored.

The Lord has words of comfort for each one of these women: «Do not be afraid; you will not suffer shame. Do not fear disgrace; you will not be humiliated. You will forget the shame of your youth. For your Maker is your Husband: the Lord Almighty is His name. The Lord will call you back as if you were a wife deserted and distressed in spirit» (Isaiah 54:4a-5a-6a). God wants to change that sadness into joy. He wants to dry each tear from their eyes. He wants them to know that although someone has failed them, there is a God in the heavens who is very real and whom they can know personally.

That woman felt like the man in the parable of the Good Samaritan: attacked, wounded, robbed, and half dead. She had been wounded in her marriage. Her husband was the thief of her happiness. Not for a day, nor a week but for years. When she finally made the decision to divorce him, she was half dead. In such conditions, Jesus—our Good Samaritan—found her and gave her the love that she had never known. He disinfected her emotional wounds with His own blood, poured the balm of His Spirit over her, and carried her to a Christian congregation so that she could receive all of the spiritual care that she needed.

LEARNING TO BE KIND TO YOUR PARTNER

When we are with someone who we like, we try to be on our best behavior in order to try to impress the person. Nevertheless, many people think that being kind to your partner is a sign of weakness. That is so far from reality! Remember that one of the basic principles of marriage: «Husbands, love your wives, just as Christ loved the church and gave himself up for her» (Ephesians 5:25). We should take our kindness to extremes in order to be ready to give life to the person that we love.

DO NOT ALLOW THE MAN TO BE «MACHO»

Even though I have always tried to be kind to you, there was a moment when my attitude was not very good because I thought that the only way to have authority in the home was to break your will so that you would do whatever I told you to do. But the Lord did not allow me to walk far down that road. One day, I asked you to iron a shirt for me for the following day. Then you told me very softly, «You have hands; you go and do it.»

That was a big blow for someone who wanted to enroll in the school for macho men.

So the next day, I told you in an even stronger tone, «I need you to get my suit ready for me for tomorrow.» With even more firmness and authority, you told me, «You have hands; you go and do it.» I was completely unsettled. Then I prayed and I told the Lord, «God, I am unsettled because my wife is not submitting to me. Help me, Lord! I am losing the authority in my home!»

Immediately, I heard the voice of God say, «Do you want to be the authority in your home?»

«Of course, Lord,» I responded. «That is my greatest desire.»

«Who is the person with the most authority that you know?» He asked me.

«Jesus Christ,» I answered.

«How did He get this authority: being served or serving?»

«Serving,» I said.

«Whom did He serve?»

«His church,» I said. «He even washed His disciples' feet and told them, 'I have not come to be served but to serve.'»

Then the Lord told me, «Go and do the same with your wife.»

This encounter produced a complete change in my thinking, a renewal of my mind. I began immediately to serve you as the Lord served His church. The following day, I brought coffee to you in bed because I had understood that kindness is closely linked to service. A week later, your attitude was very different. With such sweetness you came up to me and asked me, «My love, what do you want me to get ready for you for tomorrow?»

The Lord made me see that you did not want to negate my authority; you simply did not agree with my way of asking you to do things. Today, I thank God for not allowing that bad macho attitude to enter our home. The Lord's instruction is completely the opposite of that because being macho is an attack on kindness.

I am completely sure that if men truly understood the way that Jesus related to His church, we would try to improve our attitudes towards our wifes. And this would bring more peace and happiness to every family. Men know how to make life pleasant for our spouses, but we also know how to complicate their lives. Let us not forget that kindness is a command from the Lord: «Husbands, love your wives, just as Christ loved the church and gave himself up for her» (Ephesians 5:25). That same letter also tells us, «Get rid of all bitterness, rage and anger, brawling and slander, along with every form of malice. Be kind and compassionate to one another, forgiving each other, just as in Christ God forgave you» (Ephesians 4:31-32). Obviously, this passage can also apply to married life.

Your way of relating with your partner also reflects in all other areas of your life. Giving room to kindness will leave bitterness out and all that results from bad character. "Many a man claims to have unfailing love, but a faithful man who can find?" (Proverbs 20:6).

FREE YOURSELF FROM THE STIGMA OF BLAMING OTHERS

Human beings are used to justifying themselves and blaming others. I remember a big disagreement that we had over the phone when we were still dating. After I hung up, many accusations against you went through my mind. It was as if a spiritual force was trying to divide us, bringing to me a distorted image of you. But I quickly realized that this could not be coming either from me or from God. I also thought, «Is it that Jesus is at the right hand of the Father accusing us when we make mistakes and asking Him to punish us?» Then I imagined the Lord interceding for each of us, saying to God, «Father, do not blame your children for their errors. Look at them through me. They have had the courage to believe in me, and I accepted these wounds because of love for them.» I also remembered that the adversary would be accusing us before the Father—as He did with Job—so that He would withhold his mercy from us. This experience opened my eyes of understanding so that I would not allow any accusing spirit to enter my mind.

HURTFUL WORDS

Sarcastic words, which are like daggers even when untrue, are sometimes spoken in marriage. One observation, the fruit of helping married couples for a long time, is that the deepest wounds have been caused by words that were spoken a long time ago, perhaps years, but still echo in a person's heart and head. Words are very powerful because they immediately activate the spiritual realm and keep hammering in our minds, able to cause serious wounds. As a result, these wounds bring resentment, hatred, and vengeance. That is why it is necessary to take authority over them, to cancel every negative word aimed at your partner and replace each one with a positive word. If we learn to use the language of faith in our homes, we will fill them with a glorious atmosphere and we will bring security and confidence to those who share it with us. Nothing spreads more happiness to a woman than that she feels loved, respected, and valued by her husband. You and I have obeyed a biblical principle by establishing the norm of not going to sleep if we are angry: «Do not let the sun go down on your anger» (Ephesians 4:26). And if we have achieved it, we are sure that everything that we set out to do will be accomplished.

PHYSICAL MISTREATMENT

For many years, husbands physically abused their wives. In recent years, the opposite is happening; wives are abusing husbands. Physical or verbal abuse is a manifestation of lack of affection in a marriage. «No one ever hated his own body but he feeds and sustains it» (Ephesians 5:29).

The best way to try to solve these unpleasant situations is to find a moment for dialogue without falling into shouting, offenses, or violence. The key is to open one person's heart towards the other and get to the root of the problem, to draw the person into repentance and to ask for forgiveness and to give the person a second chance. Applying this method will bring healing to a troubled marriage.

FORGIVENESS: A KEY WORD

In order for the blessing of God to be complete at the hour of forgiveness, it is very important to consider certain aspects of forgiveness.

Forgiving from the heart

Do you remember that time just after we got married when I offended you without realizing it, because of my immaturity? You could have gone back to your father´s house and move away from me, but you did not do any such thing. Instead, you acted with maturity in everything you did, and that made you seem even more beautiful. You have never lost control. However difficult a situation may seem, you always stay calm. Obviously, it has helped us a lot to guide so many other couples because giving them counsel has also enriched our marriage.

A public confession

The truth is that it costs something to understand how two people who say that they love each other let weeks pass without saying a word. I believe that indifference is one of the greatest tortures for human beings. That is why I will never forget that time that I caused you so much pain. It was during our first international convention, which was full of representatives from many countries. On the very day that the convention began, you and I had a disagreement. I reacted in a completely ignorant way. I know that I hurt you a lot, but I pretended that it did not matter to me. Then something happened that had never occurred before. We began the meeting with both of us upset. After the opening, I introduced one of our special invited guests, the saxophone player Charles Martin. With a special grace, this man took the audience into an extraordinary spiritual withdrawal. After that, I presented you so that you could address everyone present. I ignored what the Lord was doing in you at that moment and nearly fell out of my chair when I heard you tell the audience about our disagreement that day. I felt completely confused and ashamed, asking myself, «How will our situation matter to these 20.000 people?» But as I listened to you, I understood that God had everything under control. Your words moved me: «Dear friends...» In that moment your voice broke, and you began to cry. Later, you continued, «My husband and I had a small disagreement today and therefore he is not talking to me or paying attention to me. He is ignoring me completely, and he has made me feel very bad the whole day"- at that moment, I wanted the ground to swallow me- "but when brother Charles interpreted that precious melody, the Spirit of God spoke to me and asked me, 'Daughter, does this conflict that you are having with your husband right now hurt you?'

'Yes, Lord; it hurts a lot' I responded.

'Well I have let you go through this situation because I want to teach my children something: that is the way that they treat me. Sometimes days and even weeks pass without them speaking a word to me; they treat me as if I did not exist. If your husband's attitude from only this one day hurt you, how do you think I feel when my children do it permanently or for a long period of time?"

Because of these words the audience broke into tears. Brothers got up and sought out one another; they hugged and asked forgiveness.

God does not make mistakes, and the key to any spiritual renewal is forgiveness. Although my situation was quite embarrassing at that moment, I immediately gave thanks to god for having used it to bless thousands of people.

Burying the past

Anyone who has been offended should make a stop in the way and make the decision to forgive wholeheartedly, burying the past and proposing never to bring it up again. «And when you stand praying, if you hold anything against anyone, forgive him, so that your Father in heaven may forgive you your sins» (Mark 11:25).

True forgiveness is to forget the offense that has been committed against you. Obviously this is not easy, but it is a process that helps you mature. Remember the glorious words of the Lord Jesus Christ on the cross: «Father, forgive them for they know not what they do» (Luke 23:34). And the response to His disciple's question, «Lord, how many times must I forgive my brother who sins against me? Up to seven times?» Jesus told him, «I tell you not seven times, but seventy times seven» (Matthew 18:21-22).

When a home is established in the dimension of forgiveness, it will be a happy and restored home. James affirms that all of us offend others many times and that if someone is never at fault in what he says, he is a perfect man, able to keep his whole body under control (James 3:23). We have all made mistakes at some point in time. Perfect homes do not exist—only restored ones.

Remove all bitterness from your heart

Paul said that love suffers all (1 Corinthians 13:7). We have the capacity to endure tests because no matter how big they are, there is no offense that a human being cannot overcome. That is why we know that forgiveness is a decision.

We have an example in a couple whom we have come to appreciate a lot because we saw them helping with our meetings Sunday after Sunday. One night, when I was already at the point of going to bed, the telephone rang. The anguished voice of the husband made me shake: «Please help me; my wife has just taken some poison and does not respond or show any signs of life. She has already spent ten minutes practically dead.» I encouraged him saying, «Don't worry; I'm coming to your house right now.»

Before I left I called the prayer chain so they could cover me in intercessory prayer. About twenty minutes passed before I could get to the house, and the woman recovered in that interval of time. I began to talk with them, trying to determine why the woman had made that decision. God allowed us to get to the root of the matter: her husband had never forgiven her for being unfaithful to him in the past. He humiliated her every day, treating her like a woman on the street and shaming her in front of her children and friends. The woman's desperation was so great that the only way out that she could see was suicide.

Bitterness is like cancer: it destroys everything it touches. And the best medicine with which to eradicate it is genuine forgiveness. God did not allow this woman to die because He wanted to give her a second chance. And not only her and her husband but also to every couple that asks this of him. One of our greatest satisfactions in the ministry has been to see the results of the encounters for couples; after three days, the marriage is completely restored, and the partners want to grow together.

Forgiving yourself

Accusations and blame come from the same fountain: a demonic power that tries to make human beings feel miserable. We all have to understand that if God forgives us, then we should not accept any thought of blame. Paul said, «I thank God, whom I serve, as my forefathers did, with a clear conscience» (2 Timothy 1:3). Although Paul was not completely proud of his past—having blasphemed and persecuted believers and instigated Stephen's death—once he experienced God's forgiveness, he never felt guilty.

It is important that each marriage partner understands that forgiveness is essential, but a genuine repentance is required before it can happen and restoration can come. One of the most common problems in many marriages is that the partner who is sinning in some way tries to convince the other person that it is his or her fault. And if the marriage comes to an end, the innocent one remains weighed down with guilt, believing that he or she was the reason that the home was destroyed. The bible reminds us continually that each person is responsible for his or her own actions and that no one should carry another's guilt.

When a couple moves in the dimension of forgiveness, it is going to create a completely restored and happy home. We are aware that we all offend others with our words and that we can only reach maturity when we control our mouths. As we said before, there are no perfect homes—only restored ones.

CHAPTER 5

Fifth truth

THE POWER OF COMMUNICATION

You and I are aware that with the passing of time we have learned to communicate with each other better and better. Today I give thanks to God that this knowledge has continued to grow and has never diminished even for a minute.

When I had just met you, I used to make an effort to read the expression on your face, the look in your eyes. I have always been impressed by the way you had always looked at me with such purity, innocence, and sweetness. At the beginning, you were trying to cover up those internal riches behind the trappings of shyness. I remember the first time that you were asked spontaneously to share your testimony in front of the congregation; you were very surprised. That minute seemed like the longest one of your life. But although your comments were brief, your reaction allowed me to see certain characteristics of your personality, and it revealed to me that you always have liked to speak in public—if you are prepared.

After all those years that I have known you, I can say that you are the best communicator. Your words always edify, motivate, comfort, and close the door on any negative comments. Although the rest of the world only sees the ugly part of someone, you have the ability to find the positive side. I believe that all of this is because you have cultivated a friendship with the Holy Spirit. Your permanence together with God has brought you to the place where you can see things better than they appear to be. That is why I dare to say that I am the luckiest man in the world because you always offer me words of encouragement, nourishment and motivation. You have a special ability, and you transform problems, however big they may be, into small difficulties that are easy to resolve.

God knew that you were the ideal woman for me. When adversity touched our lives and my body collapsed after the impact of those bullets, you maintained control very calmly and spread words of life over me, saying full of authority, «Cesar, don't die!» God used you like a guardian angel. You did not let the spirit of death snatch my life away because death is nothing to discuss. But a simple word of authority was enough to break it and set it aside with the understanding that it was forbidden to enter. What a great communicator you are! You put the whole angelic realm to work in order to reprimand the spiritual forces of death that were surrounding my body for almost ten days. You know how to touch the heartstrings of God.

For many years, you always used to ask me, «How do you hear the voice of God?» No matter how much I tried to explain all the ways to you, you always remained with the question. That is why it filled me with joy during our first trip to Israel when you had barely set foot in Jerusalem and heard the voice of God for the first time. The Lord told you something very interesting: «Daughter, everything in your life up until now, even the 18 years of ministry, has been a simple preparation. Your ministry has barely begun.» The happiness of your ministerial development has grown ever since that endorsement by the Word of the Lord.

THE HAPPINESS OF GOOD COMMUNICATION

Although we are living in the information age, paradoxically, the number one problem in the majority of homes is the lack of effective communication. What can be more tragic than to see a relationship deteriorate and not be able to do anything to improve it?

Watch out for confusion!

When Solomon affirmed that wisdom builds your house (Proverbs 9:1), he referred to the importance of good communication in the heart of a family. It is impossible to build a home without that essential tool.

The tower of Babel remained unfinished; it had to be abandoned because no one understood the language of the others there. Imagine the situation. The architect has a clear idea, but no one understands it. The engineer presumes to have captured the idea and tries to transmit his thoughts to the other workers, but they are deceived and begin to abandon the job because they do not understand what he is asking them to do. I believe that in some homes, a similar situation arises. The husband thinks one thing but expresses another with his mouth, and the rest understand something different. Some of them despair and say, «Doesn't anyone in this house understand me?» When this happens, the family faces the same spirit of Babel: everything is confused.

Many people do not dare to express their feelings openly due to fear of how their spouse will react. So although they think one thing, they express another. I am completely convinced that one has to use a clear and transparent language in marriage without wounding or trying to break the will of the other partner.

DO NOT BE AN AUTHORITARIAN

Do you remember that young girl who got married so full of happiness and returned from her honeymoon with her face marked by sadness? «My husband tried to break my will,» she told us. «If I do not do whatever he wants, he treats me like a capricious rebel. He tells me how much time I should pray and how I have to do it. One day, he interrupted my devotional and said, «Stop praying already.»

«I'm not finished,» I answered.

«When I tell you to stop praying,» he replied, «You should stop doing it. Are you going to work against my will?»

Her beautiful dreams were shattered. That was how that happy and dynamic young girl felt, and sadness was trying to control the issue. But God, in His mercy, allowed us to offer counsel to her and to her husband. We gave them various guidelines so that they could reach a genuine repentance. We also made them see that the first week of marriage is one of the most important because what happens during it—with words and attitudes—determines the future of the relationship.

They recognized that words that they had directed at each other had not been appropriate; they truly repented and prayed to cancel those negative words. The next step was to speak words of faith and hope in their home.

THE POWER OF WORDS

The greatest offenses are usually committed in moments of anger or desperation. We know that out of the abundance of the heart the mouth speaks. Our words either dignify us or shame us. Sometimes men forget that a woman is like a fragile glass and that the fastest way to destroy her is to use offensive words of contempt, humiliation, or violence. Jesus taught men how to treat their wives. «Husbands, love your wives as Christ loved the church» (Ephesians 5:25). The relationship between Christ and the church is the perfect example of what a correct relationship should be like.

Jesus always protected his disciples with words of love, hope, and nourishment: «Do not be afraid, little flock, because your Father has been pleased to give you the kingdom» (Luke 12:32).

I give thanks to the Lord because He has always allowed us to cultivate good communication in our home, a constant dialogue that is always progressing.

USING WORDS THAT EDIFY

«The wise woman builds her house, but the foolish one tears hers down with her own hands» (Proverbs 14:1).

You are a wise woman, the great artisan of the home that the Lord has allowed us to build. Beloved Claudia, you have always avoided using words of complaint; you have only permitted the language of faith. Your words make well to those who suffer and to those who are surrounded by uncertainty.

When I see those precious daughters that the Lord gave us and I think about the maturity with which they speak and behave, it is a reflection of what you have planted in their lives. They all admire you and seek your advice because you always have carefully chosen words for each of them.

As for me, I love sharing with you. Experts say that the majority of couples exhaust their topics of conversation within the first year of marriage and that when children arrive the couple showers almost all of their affection on them. But that has not been the case with us. Each year, we have climbed another step on the stairway of love and knowledge. We have learned to be a team.

After the Lord, you are the most important person to me. You have become my best friend, and you know how to give me those words of nourishment that I need. They are a great balm for me because you give them in the most opportune moments, especially when I come home weighed down with problems, struggles, and difficulties. You do not look at things from the same perspective that I do but through faith. God has given you the ability to transform those great mountains into simple grains of sand. That is why I realize that the problems were not as big as I thought after sharing with you, that the adversity was something that God permitted so that we could demolish it in faith. Yes, Claudia, together we have demolished walls, conquered nations, and helped and inspired millions of people.

There are four things that I admire about you as a communicator:

You always speak from the heart.
You always speak with wisdom.
You always speak with simplicity.
You always speak with faith.

YOUR WORDS MOTIVATE

I believe that you never imagined the effect that your words would have on my life. Each compliment that leaves your lips, however insignificant it may seem, produces enormous satisfaction for me. The simple act of hearing it come from your lips is the reward that I receive after a hard job.

When I get down from the pulpit after delivering a message to the congregation, your first words are of motivation, like nourishment that floods my whole being, giving me greater self-confidence. That is why I say, «Thank you, Father, because we are doing well, and only for your glory.»

When I see your disciples and I consider the time that you have invested in them, your dedication, their great growth, the affection that they have for you, I cannot say more than, «Thank you, Lord, because this is the result of the work of a woman who planted seeds of truth. Those seeds have brought fruit and have transformed women who did not believe in themselves because they had been beaten and rejected.» You have completely changed their concept of life. Thanks to you they have learned to believe in God and to worship Him, and now they are working hard to expand Christ's kingdom.

Our daughters are also witnesses that you know how to motivate. Johanna, our first daughter, wants to be just like you. After preaching in the coliseum, which was filled to the rafters, everyone who heard her said the same thing: «It is like seeing Claudia preach; she is just like her mother.» And she is what she is because of what you planted in her. Your words of motivation have greatly impacted all of our daughters. You are a great blessing, my beloved Claudia.

YOUR WORDS BRING COMFORT

The bible tells us that the great comforter is the Holy Spirit, who is at our side, giving us words of nourishment and support. Your words are like that, creating confidence, nourishment, and support. It is so important to know how to speak words to those who are weary. Due to the crises in which we live, the world does not need any more men beating up people and leaving them along the side of the road. We need more Good Samaritans who lift the wounded up to pour wine and oil on their wounds and later carry them to an inn on horseback.

The language of the wise is the only one that gives relief to the weary. And God has given you that language, Claudia. Your advice has helped many people find relief in their struggles and conflicts through faith in the Lord Jesus.

When one of our daughters was very small, she accidentally broke a piece of our china. The girl was very confused because she did not know how you would react. But your words calmed her completely: «Don't worry about the porcelain; you are much more valuable.» Those little details have allowed each one of our daughters to be self confident.

This is also reflected in your disciples, which is already a spiritual law: what happens with your children is reflected in our disciples.

LEARNING TO USE BEAUTIFUL LANGUAGE

«Husbands, love your wives as Christ loved the church in order to present it to Himself as a glorious church» (Ephesians 5:25).

With these words, the Lord was showing men that they are the ones who should beautify their wives with words that they direct at them. If a man wants to destroy a woman completely, the fastest way to do it is with words. A woman is a fragile glass that can be broken with rough words. But words are also the fastest way to build up people. The wife is her husband's glory, and that glory is the reflection of all the words that the man has planted in her life.

Knowing that, I have forced myself over these twenty-five years to give you words of love, respect, faith, hope, and motivation every day. I have always seen you as that fragile and delicate glass, and I have tried not to hurt you ever, because offending you would hurt me more than it would hurt you. I know that you are a precious gift from God for my life, and I want to build you up with my words and actions.

LOVE SHOULD NEVER BE LACKING

Love is the basis of everything. There are people who count on material goods, a prestigious career, a healthy bank account, but the most important thing is missing: love.

Love is the key word for the home, the only thing that should not be missing, because although our language may be quite eloquent like that of the angels, if we do not have love, we are nothing. Although we have the prophetic anointing and proclaim divine truth to the four winds, and although we have thousands of followers, if we lack love we are nothing. Although we see the hand of God move in our ministry through faith, if we do not have love, nothing matters.

THE IMPORTANCE OF OUR FAMILY

The priority should be the family —before the ministry. That has been our case, and I give thanks to God for it. I always feel good when I remember the note that I received from our daughter Manuela on Father's Day. She congratulated me and told me, «Daddy, thanks because your family has always been before the church, and that has made us feel very important.» When I read that note, I was moved because I understood that the most important thing, before saving the whole world, is our own family. As someone said, «No success, however big it may be, can hide the stain of a destroyed home.

The home is so valuable that it can only be built on love. That is why it must be the most important language in any marriage.

FIVE STEPS TO COMMUNICATION

In his book, «Why am I afraid to tell you who I am?» the family counselor John Powell describes five levels of communication:

1. *Light conversations*
2. *Actions*
3. *Ideas and opinions*
4. *Ideas and emotions*
5. *Intimate communication—the most profound level where people talk from the botton of their hearts.*

I dare to affirm that our communication has always been at the deepest level because we have talked without veils, with open hearts, without being ashamed of anything. We have deepened our thoughts, our feelings, and our faith. What God speaks to your heart, you share with me. And what God speaks to my heart, I share with you. And what we receive from the Lord together, we share with our daughters and later with our disciples. What a blessing.

COMMUNICATION IS A FORTRESS IN THE MIDST OF TESTS

It never ceases to amaze me that there are people who use certain texts from the bible to hide their failure to take responsibility. It is important that each person understands that the bible has given us the tools that are necessary to achieve prosperity.

The Lord said clearly that every home goes through three types of tests:

1. ***Floods.*** Floods are the adjustments of the first years of marriage.
2. ***Rivers.*** Rivers are the stages of financial testing: it is the struggle against debts and the different seasons of economic crisis. These rivers have drowned many marriages.
3. ***Winds.*** The winds are the dangers of sexual impurity and infidelity to which marriages are exposed. These usually happen when marriages have begun to stabilize. This is the test of fire, but if a person passes through it successfully, the marriage will be greatly strengthened.

But if people have built their foundations on the rock of the Word, they will not be affected by any of this.

When a couple clings to the Word, they will be able to endure adversity. You and I faced economic struggles during the first six years of marriage. God barely supplied for us; we only had just enough to live. But you never pressured me, made demands of me, or criticized me. Instead, you treated me with the same sweetness that had always been characteristic of you, knowing that our marriage was built on the word of faith and that God was going to provide for us some day.

Thanks to you being a woman of faith, the Lord gave us His blessing. We passed through tests, waters, fire, and now we are in conditions where we can help many people. We have seen the Lord's endorsement in that.

SPEAKING THE SAME LANGUAGE

When the apostle Paul said, «Do not be unequally yoked with unbelievers» (2 Corinthians 6:14), he was warning couples so that they could avoid problems, insisting that they enjoy the same spiritual affinity.

One of my sisters went through a test of faith with a young man who liked her. Everything appeared to be fine because he attended the church, he had a career, and it all seemed right. But I realized that he did not have the same potential as a leader that my sister had. So I spoke with both of them, and I told them that I did not agree with the relationship because he was not at the same spiritual level that my sister was. The man smiled and told me in a joking tone, «I know that you do not like our relationship, pastor, but we are going to continue with our desires whether you like it or not because we love each other and one day we are going to get married.» But since I knew that this relationship was not appropriate, I began to pray so that the enemy would not upset the leadership in my sister's life. The Lord responded a short time later: God opened the veil and unmasked that man who was not living as a pure Christian and had a great weakness—women. My sister saw the true person. Today, my sister has a precious home, and she and her husband are leading the youth ministry, enjoying God's incredible, supernatural endorsement.

CHAPTER 6

Sixth truth

BUILDING A GENERATION FOR GOD

THE HAPPINESS OF MARRIAGE

One of the most exciting moments that a person experiences is his or her wedding day. God puts Himself in charge of uniting two different people, and He gives them His blessing so that they can work together to fulfill their dreams.

This is what I felt: that God had prepared our meeting beforehand and that He later led us into marriage. I even remember the day that we got married. That moment was very special because I felt that God was present in our union and that He was fusing our souls, our emotions, our desires, and our bodies into one with the skill of an expert surgeon.

I felt so united with you that having you by my side was as if I had received from God a strong dose of energy through you in order to advance and face the different circumstances of life. At the same time, I understood that God was uniting us so that we could build a generation for Him together. That implied that we would influence both our physical and spiritual descendants, that we would become an example for our children so that they could impact cities, nations, and entire generations with God's favor.

The words of Solomon became reality in my life: «He who finds a wife finds what is good and receives favor from the LORD» (Proverbs 18:22). This verse could be paraphrased based on the experience that we have had in our marriage. «I found the wife that God had for me. Through her, the blessing of God has been fulfilled. He blessed me with the best woman, with a great friend, with the most excellent mother, and an exceptional leader.» When we feel fulfilled in marriage, we are ready to raise up a generation that will live in the fear of God.

THE PLANS OF GOD

In order to bring forth His plans, the Father always chooses a man and reveals to him His will and His purpose because God dreams are to develop through those men, families committed to Him. But if these people move out of the divine plan, God cannot count on them, and they become easy targets for the enemy.

God spoke through the prophet Malachi, «Has not the LORD made them one? In flesh and spirit they are his. And why one? Because he was seeking godly offspring. So guard yourself in your spirit, and do not break faith with the wife of your youth « (Malachi 2:15). The question of the prophet was, «Has not the Lord made them one, having abundance of the Spirit in Him?» This is the foundation on which the family is built upon. We know that it is not the will of God for homes to disintegrate or for couples, living under the same roof, to give opportunity for hatred and mutual offenses to enter the relationship. On the contrary, God created us to love each other, to protect each other, to care for each other, and to bless each other. Someone may ask, «Why can't we have more than one partner?» Because God, who is very wise, chose only one woman for the man and only one man for the woman. And if couples live by the principles established in His Word, there will not be any friction. I know that this verse has been a reality in our marriage.

THE STRENGTH OF LOYALTY

These twenty-five years have been the best of my life. Together, we have faced adversity, directed our daughters, taught our disciples, loved those who hated us, as well as blessing them and praying for them. But on top of everything, we have learned to surrender our lives to the service of God. We have completely submitted to Him as a family so that He can build through our lives the generation about which He dreamed of having one day.

The only thing that would interrupt the process of building a generation for God is marital infidelity. The Lord warned against this through the prophet: «Do not betray the wife of your youth» (Malachi 2:15).

Every human being must confront difficult and adverse situations. Each person passes through the test of temptation. But the Lord wants each person to work hard on preserving the home and not to make impulsive decisions because the home is worth a lot. When a family is destroyed, the possibility that the children will continue the blessing of God falls to the ground.

The Father has prepared everything so that we can reproduce His character in our children. When the home is full of harmony among family members with respect, love, and faithfulness present, the children will see this and they will feel secure. They will be able to grow without wounds or trauma or future resentment. They will feel motivated to consecrate their lives to serving God in ministry, knowing that it is possible with the help of God.

LEARNING TO BE A FATHER

God had to help me be a father because I lacked the guidance of a natural one who would explain to me how to educate my daughters since my father left this world when I was ten years old. That was one of the saddest moments of my life because it shattered my dreams of enjoying the attention from this father that he always gave to my older siblings. When he decided to dedicate himself more to his family and not travel so much—canceling commitments that would require him to be out of the city—an accident took his life away.

My older siblings' attitude was positive because they tried to fill that great void that was created, and this brought greater unity to the family, but we still felt that something was missing. When I met Jesus, He let me have an intimate relationship with the Father, who filled all of the voids in my life.

I remember that on one occasion when I was praying in my room, I took advantage of the silence and the darkness of the night, I started talking to God with great fear because I thought that He was a stern God who repaid mistakes with punishment. Fearfully, I tried to draw near to Him, thinking that at any moment He was going to punish me for my mistakes. But I soon heard a sweet voice, tender and compassionate, that told me, «Who told you that God is like that? Maybe you don't know that He is waiting with open arms for you to throw yourself into them?» When I heard that voice, I understood that it was God who was talking to me. In an act of faith, I decided to throw myself into the arms of that God who spoke to me at night, and for the first time I felt very secure. All of the emotional void that was left in my life through the loss of my father disappeared in a moment. The single act of being in the arms of God brought such peace and happiness to my heart that I never again felt any loneliness or sadness over having lost my father at such and early age.

THE PRIVILEGE OF FATHERHOOD

What a privilege it was for Adam to have God as his father. But the first man let the best opportunity of raising up a generation for God, slip away. When he opened his heart to disobedience, it brought on him a great stain that extended through all of his descendants, from generation to generation. The whole human race fell away from God. Adam's ways were so corrupt that God intervened and decided to wipe off all the creatures that He had created from the face of the earth because they had all been corrupted and their thoughts were only bad. God turned away from regretted having made man.

But Noah found favor before the eyes of God, and he and his family were used by God to preserve the human race. When God called Noah, He made a covenant with him and told him the desire of His heart for Noah and his descendants; if they lived under that covenant and submit to His laws, He would bless them from generation to generation.

But with the passing of years, it began to happen again: Noah's descendants turned away from God, who had to choose another man—Abraham—to whom He said, «Leave your country and your people and your parents' household and go to the land that I will show you, and I will make you into a great nation» (Genesis 12:1-2).

Abraham believed God and obeyed. He left his country and his parents' household. Even though he did not have a set course or a map or any kind of planned or detailed organization for his trip, he simply obeyed. His plan was whatever God told him, and he would move according to whatever the voice of God told him to do. He would do everything that God told him. Abraham learned to hear God and to obey each of His Words. And although he and his wife did not have children, God was so pleased with them that He did a miracle. He changed the way things looked and made Abraham a father of nations. Abraham had the strength of faith, and it helped him to raise a generation in the fear of God.

When our first daughter was born, I felt like my responsibility was to educate her in the fear of the Lord. Not wanting to have distorted information about fatherhood, I decided to go to the fountain: the Word of God, knowing that in His pages I would obtain the right information. I understood that I should discipline, not to wound but to form. God blessed us with girls, who require much more tender and delicate treatment. But this was not a difficult job because they were motivated by my caresses and words of affection, and we have successfully established true bonds of love and friendship with each of them.

THE MIRACLE OF REJUVENATION

God rejuvenated Abraham and Sarah. He gave Sarah strength to conceive, and He gave Abraham not only Isaac but the opportunity to call him a friend. The Lord said, «Shall I hide from Abraham what I am about to do? Abraham will surely become a great and powerful nation, and all nations on earth will be blessed through him. For I have chosen him, so that he will direct his children and his household after him to keep the way of the LORD by doing what is right and just, so that the LORD will bring about for Abraham what he has promised him» (Genesis 18:17-19). God predetermined Abraham's future: father of a great and mighty nation, fountain of blessing for all the nations of the earth. Why? Because Abraham became a true father, and this is the closest thing to God's heart. A good father instructs his children and establishes his home in the ways of God; that is what Abraham did with his descendants. You and I, Claudia, parents of four daughters, are the most privileged to see that they all love God and want to reproduce themselves in others to extend God's work.

I FEEL LIKE THE LUCKIEST FATHER

I am one of the luckiest men on the face of the earth because God has adorned our home with four princesses, and He has allowed me to see how they have each developed in the ministry. I have written a letter to each of our daughters, and it seems appropriate to reproduce them here.

Letter to Johis

My dear Johanna,

I am so happy to hear you preach with eloquence and the wisdom of God. The brothers have shared how they have been blessed by your teaching. When you were standing on the platform, full of authority in front of the audience, no one wanted to miss even one syllable of your words, this helped me to see the transformation that God had caused in you. Your heart has changed so much, making you a tremendous servant of God who enjoys a strong union with the Holy Spirit.

Although we were always sure of that anointing upon your life, it never ceases to amaze us how quickly the Lord has worked in you. It is not normal to see such a big congregation become broken and desire to restore their relationships with God. What is your secret? I believe that there are various aspects, and one of them is that you were filled with the Holy Spirit since you were in your mother's womb. Another is that you kept yourself for God and decided to be a woman of the covenant, a covenant that you have always kept. You are a pastor through and through; you have learned what it means to love souls, and you have protected the fruit that God has given you. Just like a mother gives her whole heart to caring for her children, you have given yourself to caring for the people whom the Lord has entrusted to you. You have an open mind to the revelation of the Word, and that makes it very easy for you to see the revelations that the Spirit brings into your life.

Johis, you have always been so mature and your decisions so firm that your sisters admire you, your disciples imitate you, your husband praises you, and your parents are proud of you. You are our Johis (gift from God); you are like a beautiful jewel that shines on every side. You have strength to conquer, and you have always refused easy challenges. I know that you have the same anointing as Abraham and that you will be able to touch the families of the earth through your ministry. You also have the anointing of a pastor, a prophet, and a writer.

Daughter, I am taking this opportunity to tell you that I love you and that I am very proud of you. I love, respect you, admire you, and I am happy to be your father.

Cesar C.

Letter to Lorena

None of your sisters received as many presents as you did on the day you were born. Your mother and I realized that your arrival signified financial blessing for our home. You came right when we needed that blessing the most, that is why we called you Lorena (woman praised).

When the Lord created you, He also was careful to maintain communication between your emotions and your spirit. That is why you have a special ability to touch the heart of God through worship. The adversary had planned to snatch your parents from you on that day of your birthday, but the Lord did not let him. God intervened and transformed the curse into blessing.

Since then, I have witnessed that the anointing of God has grown in you. The words that come out of your mouth have so much power that they put the angelic realm to work. God has raised you up in order to bring His presence to this earth. When you minister, the anointing of God falls over the people, and even the most introverted cannot hold back their tears. You are a prophet of God because the anointing remains on you.

I know that God has given you big dreams. You do not look at the size; you look at the Lord, so you are very special for Him and He always has more to give to you than you have to ask of Him. God will endorse everything that you touch and undertake. You will have the ministry that you desire, and you will be able to go wherever your faith carries you. Remember the words of Paul, «No eye has seen, no ear has heard, no mind has conceived what God has prepared for those who love him» (1 Corinthians 2:9). Hold onto your dreams; build your faith; and use the voice of authority.

That is the prayer of a father who loves you and feels like the most privileged man to have you as a daughter.

Cesar C.

Letter to Manuela

God has very special ways of surprising us with blessings, and that was what I felt when you were born because you are a precious gift from heaven. Your mother and I understand that you represent the ministerial blessing and therefore that you should be called Manuela (God with us). You have brought such happiness to our home that is really is a privilege to have you in it. When God was forming you in your mother's womb, He skillfully implanted tenderness in your emotions.

This is the most outstanding characteristic of your personality; that is why it has been very easy for you to develop in ministry because you have a special ability to attract other followers as well as the authority to forge their character. Your mind and your heart are like sponges that absorb the greatest truths from the revelation of the Word in order to invest it later in your disciples. You also have a strong anointing as a pastor and teacher of the Word.

Manuelita, to believe is something very easy for you, inherent in your personality, because you have learned to look beyond the circumstances. In the most difficult moment that we had as a family, when you saw bullets enter my body, your faith never wavered. And you told one of your aunts in a moment of great commotion for her, «Don't worry; if the Lord has freed my dad from so many adversities, He will free him from this one.» Those words could only spring from a heart full of faith.

You have already seen for yourself that faith changes the most complicated predictions. When you were ten years old, they diagnosed you with septic arthritis. But after praying for you, the circumstances changed immediately. This change confused the doctors completely. Seven doctors examined you in one day because they were in shock over the manifestation of such a palpable miracle.

The Lord allowed you to go through this because He was already marking the nature of your ministry. God is going to use you in healings, signs, and wonders. Stay in the Word; cultivate your relationship with the Spirit of God; develop the steps of your vision, and this will keep you on the path until it is God's time for you. You are the prophet of God. The anointing of spiritual warfare is on you, which will allow you to discern and destroy the forces of evil that operate in the air. With every gesture that you make, with each word that you say, with each prayer that you lift, the demonic powers are broken, the heavens are cleansed, and the atmosphere is prepared so that hearts can receive the Word. The Lord wants to give you nations because, just like Ruth, you will be able to raise up a generation for God. That is the prayer of a father who loves you.

Cesar C.

Letter to Sara

You were born months after your mother became a senator; therefore, everyone called you «the little senator.» And years later, God gave your mother a prophetic word: «You youngest daughter has the anointing of the father and the mother; she will do both.» The Lord had already laid out your personality: the strength of the authority combined with tenderness. That is why we called you Sarah (princess). The Lord gave you a spirit of conquest because it is what is necessary to develop the ministry that God has prepared for you.

With great pleasure, I remember that experience when you were six years old. You took me to a shopping center, showed me a motorcycle for children, and you asked me to buy it for you. When they told me the price—$800—I said, «That toy is too expensive for you.» You did not insist but when we went to another store you asked me to buy you a purse for $10. I told you that I would because it seemed reasonable. When you had the purse in your hands, you asked me for ten dollars and when I gave them to you, you told me, «From now on I am starting to save money to buy my motorcycle.» I knew that you were daring, but I did not know that you would go so far. That same day, you asked your grandparents and your uncles for $10. Later, you did the same thing with my twelve, and even later with your mother's twelve, and later with the twelve from the youth network. In a matter of a week, you had collected enough money. It was something incredible. I realized that since then you were marking the nature of your ministry. That is why I told you, «Sara, God has given you the gift of faith. It will not be hard for you to fulfill your dreams; you will be able to have whatever ministry you desire and grow as much as you want because you are a person of faith.» And now I add this: Prepare yourself as best you can; cultivate friendship with the Holy Spirit; develop every step of your vision; make sure that the Lord Jesus Christ is always your model. If you do that, you will be able to develop a supernatural ministry.

With much love from a father who is blessed by such a special daughter.

Cesar C.

Letter to Eliemerson

For us, it is a great privilege to count you as one of our children because we feel so close to you as if you had grown up with us. You are a blessing, not only for our daughter Johanna but also for the whole family. You are that precious jewel, guarded by the Lord and manifested in this time. Thanks for letting us be your family. Thanks for letting us consider you as a son because although we never had a boy, you are as valuable as seven of them.

We know that it was not easy for you to leave your country and your home to face another culture and a new language without knowing if you would be rejected or accepted. But you moved, compelled by that faith that you have always had. I know that the hand of God worked in your heart during your years of living alone because He was waiting for the time when you would join your life with Johanna's. Together in the hands of God, you two are as powerful as dynamite, just as the Word teaches: «A thousand will flee in the presence of one; in the presence of two, ten thousand will flee» (Isaiah 30:17).

You have the anointing of conquest, and just as the Lord told Joshua, «I will give you every place where you set your foot, as I promised Moses» (Joshua 1:3), God will show you what you need to conquer. That is why it is important for you to strengthen yourself in Him and try to do what the Lord has told you. Since your birth, God has inspired your parents to mark the nature of your life with the name that they gave you: Eliemerson (God is my wisdom). That is why I am completely sure that each one of your steps has been laid out beforehand by divine wisdom. The closest thing to the heart of God is the character of a father, and you have such a heart. That is why I am sure that God will give you grace in order to bless many.

May the Lord give you the best products of the earth, the best children, and the most anointed ministry. For me, it is a privilege to count on you now, not only as a son but also as my disciple.

Cesar C.

THE SATISFACTION OF BEING A FATHER

When I saw Johanna pastoring the youth, Lorena ministering in praise, Manuela guiding and forming her disciples, and Sarah ministering in dance and worship, the only thing I could say was, «Thank you, Lord, for letting us build a generation for You.» Our daughters are so sure of themselves, so firm in their decisions, so clear in their goals that I enjoy watching the fruit of what we have planted in them as parents.

It is a blessing to feel the presence of God when Lorena ministers to the Lord's heart through music and to see how she also has been able to grow in cell groups and in disciples, teaching them week after week. This reminds me of a memorable experience that I had the day that she turned 14.

I took her to dinner at an expensive restaurant, and it was one of the greatest satisfactions of my life. When we had sat down, she asked me, «Daddy, wasn't it better to eat with the whole family?»

I answered her, «All of us are always together, but just the two of us very few times, and this is a great chance to share.»

We began to talk heart to heart. I opened mine to Lorena and told her, «Sweetheart, I have a lot of occupations. You know the commitments and the activities of the ministry. Many times a person thinks he is working correctly when it is not so, but the rest are the ones who realize it. Daughter, what would you like me to change?»

My daughter sat there surprised by this question and replied: «No, daddy, I like how you are.»

I continued, «Maybe you need me to dedicate more time to you.»

«No, daddy, the truth is that we share a lot. The last few years, we have shared enough as a family and we believe that that frequency is okay.»

That response filled me with satisfaction because I felt like I had passed the test of fatherhood with her and that my daughter did not feel like I was neglecting her.

So many parents never give their children adequate space so that they can talk and express what is in their hearts. I am more than convinced that it is very important to listen to their opinions about us.

Our conversation did not end there because I took the opportunity to seal a promise with her between father and daughter. I told her, «Daughter, you are entering into a precious age, and you are becoming very beautiful because that is what happens at your age. It is normal that you will feel attracted to the opposite sex, but I want you and I to make a pact today, a pact that will bring protection to your life and happiness to our home: I want to ask you not to make any emotional commitment before you turn 18.»

Lorena opened her eyes at me and said, «Daddy, how old was my mother when she married you?» Of course her mother got married before she was 18. And I responded to her, «Sweetheart, that was another time.» We were sharing like that until she told me, «Okay, daddy, I won't make an emotional commitment to anyone before I turn 18.»

«The second thing I want you to promise me is that it will only be to a Christian man with a testimony and leadership.»

Our daughter answered me, «Okay, daddy.»

And I continued, «And the third thing is that you will never do anything in secret, that you will never hide a relationship from us, but that when you like a boy you are going to introduce him to us openly because we will always be here to advise you and guide you.»

She told me, «Ok, daddy.»

We held hands and I prayed over our pact and commitment. After sharing that dinner, I noticed that the affection of my daughter towards me increased. She became more caring because she realized that her father valued her so much.

RESTORING FATHERHOOD

Today, fatherhood is in crisis. The world is crying out for the restoration of fatherhood: that the man be the true spouse, the true father, the true protector, the true provider, that he does not abandon his children, that he does not turn his back when they need him most.

I remember the case of a youth who was used to standing on the corner only one block from our home. He was in front of one of the best houses in the area, holding some kind of drug in his hand. One day, I went up to him to share about Jesus. His reaction was to tell me, «Look, the truth is that nothing matters to me.»

And he pointed at the house: «I live in that beautiful house. My dad is a business man who has a lot of money. But every time I tell him, 'dad, I have to talk to you,' his only response is to give me money. And when I try to talk with my mother, she tells me, 'son, I can't help you now because I have a commitment with my friends.' My parents never have had time for me.» He continued, «That is why I take refuge in this vice, which has become my friend and companion.» We talked a little longer. I wanted this young person to know Jesus. I realized that this boy is an example of the crisis of our whole society.

The scripture says that no one can enter into the house of a strong man and take his goods unless he first binds him (Matthew 12:29). Sadly, many parents are bound by vices, greed, exaggerated desires to be rich, or impure or uncontrolled passions. Then the enemy comes in and confuses the wife and children. Today more than ever, we need to see restored family values.

The father is like the captain of a ship: if he makes a mistake, he can destroy the whole ship. God has placed us as pilots of our families. That is why we should have very good communication with the control tower. In other words, we need to strengthen our relationship with the Holy Spirit so that everything we do is guided by Him. The Lord said through the prophet Hosea, «My people are destroyed from lack of knowledge. 'Because you have rejected knowledge, I also reject you as my priests; because you have ignored the law of your God, I also will ignore your children' (Hosea 4:6). The father is the priest of each home, and if he forgets to teach his children the law of God, He also will forget his children.

PLANTING THE BEST IN OUR CHILDREN

«Do not be deceived: God cannot be mocked. A man reaps what he sows» (Galatians 6:7).

Paul reminds us of the importance of planting and harvest. This image can also be applied to families because whatever we plant in them is what we will harvest. The crisis in which our whole society is immersed has affected the family. The influence of the media has been devastating to family relationships. There are many homes where each member of the family is self-sufficient; there is no uniform criteria for work or to face different areas of life.

But God has given us a strong desire to work for the restoration of families. We have come to the conclusion that the best protection for families is a marriage where the partners work as a team in the ministry. There are no problems if both partners participate in secular activities because God also can use them in ministerial areas. This produces a powerful effect in the children because they feel committed to being there and to be part of what their parents are doing.

Something that we have understood is that we should plant good things in our children: planting the best things in them now in order to harvest the best actions from them tomorrow. It is now a good opportunity to remembering some of the areas where we have planted together in our daughters.

WE PLANT POSITIVE ATTITUDES

You and I know how important it is to use positive language. This should be the language of faith because it does not allow people to be influenced by their circumstances but rather they learn to speak the Word of God and to express divine counsel. Every word given by God encourages us towards success.

I enjoy seeing the relationship that you have with our daughters. More than a mother, they see you as a great friend, and they treat you with the same confidence as if you were another sister. They always come to you when they need something or when they are going through a difficult moment. And you always have words of encouragement for them. It seems that you erase their problems from their minds when they talk to you. Your responses carry the anointing of God. You present the most adverse thing as something simple and passing. And the truth is that it is like that because after taking authority over the issue, whatever it is, and beginning to take the right steps, they understand that the greatest difficulties are inside themselves. Thank in large part to your example, our daughters are like Joshua and Caleb, always in the vanguard, always with the spirit of conquest.

In our four daughters, we have a sample book of temperaments. Lorena was the most sensitive. I have really enjoyed seeing the change that God has worked in her: now she is a woman of faith, vision, and goals. It has all been because of your help.

WE PLANT INTEGRITY

When our children are not able to see God, the first impression that they will have about the Creator is through their parents. If the parents treat each other with mutual respect and maintain harmony, the children will feel confident about drawing near to the Almighty God. They will feel motivated to follow the steps of their progenitors. The life of integrity is a life of intimate relationship with God and with His Word. Whoever accepts the divine laws will not break the human ones.

WE PLANT SPIRITUALITY

Although we know that salvation is not something hereditary but rather a personal commitment to God, you and I have forced ourselves to create an atmosphere that is conducive to our daughters feeling motivated to give their lives to Jesus. God has rewarded our effort because each one of them, in her moment, has made the decision to follow the Lord Jesus Christ. They have been totally personal and voluntary decisions. I enjoy seeing them all serve God whole-heartedly and seeing Him give them fruit in their ministries.

As parents we had to make decisions that would help our daughters to develop themselves in ministry. When Johanna was an adolescent she asked me, «Daddy, I want you to disciple me.» To me, it seemed like an excuse for her not to get involved in youth activities at the church. So I said to her, «Sweetheart, there is a whole ministry dedicated to youth. I prefer that you integrate yourself into that ministry because they know how to treat youth. It is better that you are with them.»

Johanna accepted it and did that with great enthusiasm. That ministry contributed to the formation of her character, placing the necessary bricks so that she could be the leader that she is today. And the example of the oldest daughter is important because it marked the behavior of the others. Thanks to Johanna, our daughters saw how it was the most normal thing in the world to join the youth ministry. They all learned to have a daily prayer time and to fill their notebooks from studying the Word. On some occasions, I have read the notes from their devotionals, and I have been pleasantly surprised to see how much revelation is in those pages.

WE PLANT DISCIPLINE

Discipline is to give them direction, not to hurt them or create traumas. Discipline is the brake that stops the uncontrolled urges of the human being. Solomon said that the child is born with the foolishness inherent in his nature, but the rod of discipline, direction, correction will drive this defect from him (Proverbs 29:11). The author of Hebrews taught that no discipline is good for the present but it later bears peaceful fruit (Hebrews 12:11). And any child who does not have to endure discipline is not a legitimate child but a bastard (Hebrews 12:8). Whoever does not educate his children abhors them, but he who loves them disciplines them from an early age.

You and I have not disciplined our daughters with a firm rod but with a loving, understanding, caring, guiding rod. Therefore, they not only admire and obey you but they want to imitate you in everything.

WE PLANT A CORRECT IMAGE

Upon seeing the development of our daughters, I realize that you have been like a guardian angel for each one of them because each time that they have allowed thoughts that go against their self-image or in the occasion when they have complained about the circumstances, you have used your special ability to make them see their error. As a result, none of them ever accepts an incorrect self-image in even the smallest things.

If we destroy the image of ourselves that God has given us, we not only kill our dreams and hopes but we also enter into complete disadvantage on the highway of this world; it will seem to us that all the rest are much more advanced than we are. But each word that has left your lips, each attitude, each expression, each teaching has been added together so that our daughters have a balanced self-image.

We know that the strongest wounds suffered by human beings have been caused within the family. And in general, love itself has been damaged and also the self-esteem and feelings. The wounds have been so big that many find themselves as people who are like the Good Samaritan in the parable who was wounded, robbed, and abandoned by the side of the road.

Something that we have forced ourselves to do as parents is

never to touch the self-esteem of our children. Each human being has his own dignity, and if it is trampled, one does not have anything to cling to and remains unprotected and abandoned. For that reason, there are people who feel that their lives do not have meaning because their souls are wounded and their hearts have been broken. To wound someone's self-esteem is like taking the person out of his place of refuge and leaving him completely unprotected. We also have to be aware that values change with age. What is insignificant for a young person can be the biggest thing to a child. What is important to a young person can be insignificant to an adult. That is why parents should have wisdom in order not to wound the self-esteem of their children.

In this process it is very important to learn not to blame others. Integrity consists of not admitting any reproach against your neighbor, against your own offspring. Who are the closest people to us? Our children and our siblings. If we put away the accusing finger and learn the language of forgiveness, the atmosphere of the home will change completely. «A man's wisdom gives him patience; it is to his glory to overlook an offense» (Proverbs 19:11). It is a question of simply following the example of Jesus who told the adulterous woman, «Neither do I condemn you; go and sin no more» (John 8:11). Jesus' secret was to use love to convince people of their errors.

MORE GOLDEN RULES TO EDUCATE OUR CHILDREN

Do not despise others

There is nothing more displeasing to a person than to be treated with disdain, as if he were an object of little value. Do you want to show contempt for your children? Then talk to them about the effort that you are giving for them; remind them how much you have to work so they can study, eat, and have a roof over their heads. Maybe you believe that this is something positive, but it is completely the opposite because your children will think, «Who told you to have children if you can't take care of them, if they are going to be a burden to you?» Our children are very sensitive and want everything that parents do to be out of love and generosity.

Avoid comparisons

A child feels very bad when the parents lift him up to his brothers and sisters as an example: «Do you see, son? You are no good for anything! But your brother is. Try to be more like your brother.» The result of comparison will be more rebellion.

Do not ignore them

We all like for people to pay attention when we speak. If our children see that we do not take their words into account, that we hardly greet them when we get home, that we ignore them, we are throwing painful darts at their hearts. As a result, they will try to fill that lack of affection and love in some other way. They will probably do it with methods that are not appropriate.

Bless your children

What a beautiful moment it was when we understood how as parents we should bless our daughters, the way the patriarchs of old did. What an astonishing discovery that the blessing of God is integral because it covers the spiritual, the physical, and the economic.

You and I use the same blessing with our daughters that Isaac used for Jacob. When Isaac smelled the clothing of Jacob, he blessed him (Genesis 27:27-29). I appropriated that idea, and I told each of our daughters: you smell like a field that the Lord has blessed. May God give you of heaven's dew and of earth's richness- an abundance of grain and new wine. May nations serve you and peoples bow down to you. Be lord over your brothers, and may the sons of your mother bow down to you. May those who curse you be cursed and those who bless you be blessed.

When we released this blessing over our daughters, the presence of God was such that I felt like that same day their hearts were completely transformed, becoming hearts of conquerors. It seemed that the power of the Almighty came over their lives and lifted them to a higher level of anointing. It was as if we had activated the entire angelic realm, putting it to work for them. It was as if we had given an order to the hosts of evil not to touch them because they are under the protection of God.

It was like setting forth the road on which they should walk. It was to present to them with clarity the future that awaited them.

When a father blesses his children, the blessing touches his lips before it touches them. The same thing happens with a curse: the curse touches the lips of the father first. This means that we can curse our children. The Lord taught us that so that we would bless and not curse. Our children definitely have to struggle from day to day against many adverse forces in the spiritual world. What they least want to hear, therefore, are rough words and curses. They want to receive words of blessing. Therefore, parents should always prepare an atmosphere that is conducive to continually blessing their children.

CHAPTER 7

Seventh truth

We Decided to be Guided by the Spirit of God

KNOWING THE HOLY SPIRIT

Since the day I met you, I have been sure that your life as well as mine would be guided by the Spirit of God. As family, we decided that the Holy Spirit would be the most important part of our lives and that whatever we would do would be for His glory. And just as the spirit of man knows the deepest or hidden things, the Holy Spirit knows the most intimate, the deepest, the secret parts of God's heart, and we have not received the spirit of the world but the spirit of God.

Humans are beings with intelligence that have, feel, and express emotions. They laugh and cry and get sad. Well, the Holy Spirit has those same characteristics. When someone sins, the Holy Spirit is saddened; when someone obeys, the Holy Spirit is glad, and when someone is going through a test, the Holy Spirit has sympathy for that person.

Previously, I had the wrong idea that God was not interested in our difficult moments. But a veil was removed from my eyes when I read Isaiah 63:9: «In all their distress he too was distressed, and the angel of his presence saved them. In his love and mercy he redeemed them; he lifted them up and carried them all the days of old.» In our afflictions, He is also afflicted. Isn't that logical if He is our father? Don't we hurt when our children are suffering? God does, too.

BE SURE OF YOUR CALLING

When I was single, I was certain that God would unite me with a woman that He chose for me because I was aware of a strong calling of the Lord on my life. But I also realized that I did not want to carry out that responsibility alone. When I met you, Claudia, I knew that we would unite our lives in serving the Lord. I was completely sure that the God that I came to know in the living room of my home, who had revealed Himself to me as in the flames of a fire and who had moved my heart in only a moment, filling me with the Holy Spirit, was not going to let me make a mistake in that area. That is why, just a short time after meeting you, I told you with great certainty that you were going to be my wife. It was something that God had already showed me. And since the day we got married, He put his agenda ahead of ours and has been directing each one of our steps.

LEARNING TO LIVE ON MANNA

Our first six years of marriage, we lived on basic provision. We longed to enjoy financial freedom, and I was striving hard in my job, but we did not see any change. We felt like the people of Israel when God sent them manna to eat in the desert. The Lord told them to collect enough for a day, but some of them who wanted to be prepared gathered enough for two days, and the bread spoiled. They had no choice but to get used to living on their daily provision.

But I never forgot that night. I had just finished preaching in the church that I used to pastor. It had been a memorable meeting, and I went home happy. Along the road, I heard the voice of the Lord: «In six days, God created the heavens and the earth, and the seventh day He rested. Those six years of marriage have been years of formation. From now on, you will enter into rest, into the highest economic blessing.»

The truth is that the financial issue never worried me much because since the Lord saved me, that was what interested me the least. But things changed when God blessed me with a family; I understood that my duty was to have a secular job in order to provide for my family, even though my heart had always been in the ministry. And as it happens with the things of God, prosperity came little by little.

WE WRITE DOWN OUR PETITIONS

I even keep that planner that we used in 1983 to write down all of our petitions, with the exact date of the moment in which we made the prayer. In another column, at the end of the line, we wrote down the day of the response. We began to ask the Lord for things—things that seemed impossible for us. We pointed at the agenda and we prayed for those requests every day. We decided to believe God, not based on what we had because we did not have anything but based on the promise that He had given us through revelation and by His Word. Within one year, the Lord responded affirmatively to 70% of the petitions that we made that day. It was all miraculous, and you and I discovered the importance of writing down our petitions and persevering until we see a response.

WE ENJOY THE BLESSING

We got our first vehicle through faith. Johanna, who had just turned six, began to pray saying, «Lord, I ask you to give my dad the car that He needs.» She also mentioned the brand because she had learned it by heart. God also used our daughter to save her grandfather. «Lord, save my grandfather and take away his desire to drink so much liquor,» she prayed. Later, she preached to him and guided him to repeat that prayer.

When we wanted to buy our own house, I saw one that I liked. Then I began to look at it and dream about it. Remember that we continually claimed it in prayer? The Lord's response was, «Do you want that house?» «Yes, Lord.» «Well you already know what you have to do: conquer it by faith.» I set myself to praying, and although I did not have oil in my hands, by faith I began to fill the whole house with oil. I visited it in the spirit and anointed it with oil saying, «No one will be able to buy this house because it belongs to me". A few months later the owner called me to offer it to me with broad payment options.

You and I are convinced that we can have access to material things because Jesus has already conquered them for us. He only waits for us to believe it and extend our hands to appropriate each promise that He has given us in His word. Do not forget that prosperity is the result of hearing the voice of God, retaining His Word and practicing it. His blessings are in the city or the country. God will bless our children, our income, our family budget, our departure from work and our return. He promised to defeat all the enemies that raise themselves up against us. Poverty is one of our enemies. Solomon said that it comes like an armed man (Proverbs 6:11), and it finds more than one of us distracted. But the counterpoint is the promise of the Lord: «The LORD will grant you abundant prosperity-in the fruit of your womb, the young of your livestock and the crops of your ground» (Deuteronomy 28:11). One of the blessings is the protection of our family, something in which God has been present this whole time.

LEARNING TO MATURE

When we were young and daring, we did a lot of unwise things by following our first impulses. But there are other moments in which the Spirit of God says, «I am going to guide you.» Remember what Jesus told Paul: «When you were younger you dressed yourself and went where you wanted; but when you are old you will stretch out your hands, and someone else will dress you and lead you where you do not want to go» (John 21:18). That is what maturity consists of—not dressing yourself the same but letting God do it; not going wherever you want but where God tells you to go. It is simply to let the Spirit of God guide and govern you. We have learned to do that, and it is truly the most exciting thing in the world.

Sometimes people feel uncertain because they are already used to a certain work supervisor. Our lives have remained crucified because that is the only way to expect the Spirit of God to speak to us and to depend completely on his direction, submitting ourselves to everything that He desires.

THE PURPOSE OF THE CALLING

When I began to take the first steps in my Christian life, I was convicted that it was important to read the bible. It was like looking at myself in a mirror because these readings showed me my spiritual condition. A burning desire was awakened in me to seek God because I realized that only He could clean my soul. The same night of my personal encounter with Jesus, I also was completely sure that God was calling me to preach the gospel, and from that point on I began to prepare myself for the ministry. It was easy at the beginning because I did not know any Christian churches and never had attended a congregation that was not the traditional church.

HOW DO WE PREPARE OURSELVES?

How can we prepare ourselves for a spiritual ministry? We have to enter into intimacy with the Spirit and allow Him to speak directly to our hearts. We will receive His advice then, in His anointing, communicating the truths that He reveals to us to our disciples.

PRAYING IN THE SPIRIT

If we succeed in entering daily into a prayer of intimate communion with the Spirit, we will never be the same again because we will renew our minds and obtain blessing for our family. We will also receive guidance for our finances and anointing for the ministry. We will enter into the secret place of God.

A few years ago, when I began to pray, I was thinking that it was normal to do it for an hour. During those sixty minutes, a fierce battle raged in my mind because it was so easy to get distracted. I was attacked by thoughts about my debts, obligations, commitments, or family. And when my mind had finally begun to calm itself, my hour of prayer was finished. One day, however, the Spirit told me, «Son, you are praying wrong. When you calm down and you believe that you have finished is when you begin to be ready to offer the kind of prayer that pleases me.» That day I asked the Lord to forgive me; I set aside my daily activities and entered into prayer in the Spirit.

AN ATMOSPHERE OF GLORY

When you go to pray in the Spirit, all of your mind should be settled down. The problems have to be set aside. The eagerness has to disappear. God needs intimacy with you and longs for us to give your whole being to Him. He wants us to leave the natural realm and enter the supernatural dimension of the Spirit.

When I understood this, I began to pray in a very different way. Not only my prayer changed but I also noticed a change in the atmosphere around me. It was like on a very hot day when you enter an air-conditioned place and feel that freshness of the moving air. That same thing happened when I crossed that spiritual barrier and entered into intimacy with God. A veil was removed, and I saw with unveiled face; I contemplated all of the greatness and the majesty of God. I saw angels ministering to Him, seraphims adoring Him, archangels serving Him continuously, surrendering their lives. The elders threw themselves before Him, gave him their crowns, and exalted Him saying, «Holy, you are holy, Lord of heaven and earth. There is no other God besides You; all of creation worships and blesses and glorifies you because you have been given a name that is above all other names. You reign in all the earth; all of creation bends its knee before you and adores you because only you are God, and all the glory, all the riches, all the honor and all the power from century to century belongs to you.»

Being in the middle of such intimate communion, not many words came to me. I could only say, «Holy, holy, holy.» While I was worshiping Him, I saw with total clarity, as in a mirror, all of His greatness, all of the splendor of God's world, all of the beauty of the celestial city, because our true city is there, with Him. God Himself designed it and built it for us. I understood then that we are spiritual beings that live in a human body, and when we enter into such intimacy with God, our spirits come to be one with the Spirit of God.

If we enter into that intimacy with God, we will never be the same again. We bless Him, we glorify Him, we exalt Him, and we understand that God is a holy being. He is not an idea or something abstract; He is a person, and we can know Him as our true Father. The greatest experiences of my life have happened in that intimacy with the Spirit because He allowed me to know the many faces of God: a father who healed my wounds, a friend in whom I can trust, the provider of all my needs. I came to be so familiar with Him that entering into His presence became the greatest desire of my life.

HOW TO TRANSFORM YOUR CIRCUMSTANCES

A while ago, when I was in Miami, God brought me a text from the Word: «On the Lord's Day I was in the Spirit» (Revelation 1:10). That verse rattled around in my mind, even when I went to bed. It followed me and turned over and over in my thoughts. I began to meditate and said, «Lord, what does it mean that John was in the spirit?» His response was very clear: «You enter the spirit when you give up your problems, your worries, your feelings, your thoughts and enter the spiritual realm, where the Almighty dwells. That is where God reveals His will.» Then I said, «Lord, I am going to be in the Spirit.» I got up and I began to pray earnestly in faith. I said, «Lord, I want to come into your presence; I want to connect my spirit with yours; I want to enter the spiritual realm where you are.» I persevered in prayer until I felt that I came into the world of God. The connection with the spirit was such that I felt like I was one with God. I saw things with other eyes because the veil was pulled back and the will of God was revealed.

SEEING THINGS BETTER THAN THEY ARE

When I was in that spiritual dimension, the twelve disciples that I was making in Miami came to my mind. I saw so many defects in them, so many problems, struggles, and difficulties. Then I asked, «Lord, is there hope for these men? If they are not adequate, would it be better to dedicate myself to making others? I do not want to waste time on people who will not bear fruit. Lord, they don't even believe in themselves!»

The Spirit of God told me, «Son, you think like that because you have always looked at them with natural eyes. They will not grow until you see that they can do it. Neither will they believe in themselves until you believe in them.» The problem was not in them but in me because I saw them according to the circumstances and not with spiritual eyes.

The truth is that the Spirit surprised me. It was the first time that I had that kind of revelation. How did the story go? I began to see them from a different perspective. By faith, I moved them from the natural world to the spiritual realm. And although they all had their faults, problems, and inadequacies, they hardly passed through the door of the spiritual barrier when I began to see them differently—transformed into tremendous leaders with thousands of disciples.

On the following day, I met with them. We prayed together and the glory of God fell in an incredible way on each one present. Those who had any type of bondage cried, repented, and moaned. That night, their hearts were completely changed and miracles happened.

I know that each believer has the opportunity to make disciples. If he does it through faith, he will be able to see them as the best leaders in the whole world. Our disciples are like our children: we should believe in them, help them to grow, and avoid hurting them with our words. Do you have disciples? Then loose the spirit of life over them, and they will produce all of the fruit in abundance that you can visualize.

SEEING THE BLESSINGS

When you think about the future of your disciples, you will also see the problems or infirmities that want to attack their lives. But God will also allow you to see His great healing power. In order for the Father to reveal to us His will, we have to spend time in His presence. God desires to reveal to them things that they have never heard or thought of. The blessing that God has prepared for us cannot be received with the natural mind because He moves by means of His Spirit. Only when you enter into an intimate relationship can God show you what is in His heart, showing you His blessings which are good, pleasing, and perfect.

SEEING THE MINISTERIAL BLESSING

Do not be afraid to serve God because He will bless you in the ministry. Maybe you are struggling to finish your studies, your work, and the ministry. Do not lose any of these things, but remember that your first objective is the ministry. Pray earnestly, cry out with your entire being, and desire to serve the Lord with all of your strength. He wants you to rescue those who are lost. Find them, take them out of their world of sin, vice, or impurity and transfer them to the kingdom of God.

In order to achieve this, you need the love of God in your heart, that love that is on top of everything, including your circumstances. Ask the Spirit of God to baptize you in His love in order to expand the kingdom of God.

SEEING ECONOMIC BLESSING

You should learn to see that God has an economic blessing for you. He is going to be faithful. For nine years, I combined my role as pastor with secular work. But when God called me to my actual ministry, he told me, «Worry about serving me, and I will worry about your needs.» I obeyed that word, and until this very day, God has never failed to keep His promise. Remember that He fulfills what He promises.

If you are faithful with the work of God, He will move the heavens in order to bless your life, your house, and your family. You will not lack any material good in this earth.

BE TRANSFORMED

We have learned to see the blessings of God as in a mirror, just as the apostle Paul expressed it by saying, «And we, who with unveiled faces all reflect the Lord's glory, are being transformed into his likeness with ever-increasing glory, which comes from the Lord, who is the Spirit» (2 Corinthians 3:18).

How does this transformation occur? Just like the transformation of a butterfly that changes from a caterpillar into a beautiful creature. When you develop intimacy with the Spirit, you can feel what is unworthy, what is full of bondage, struggling against thoughts, suffering attacks of impure desires. When you enter into intimacy with God, these things become uncomfortable and annoying. But when we successfully shed our nature and set it aside, the metamorphosis occurs. We will think about natural people as spiritual ones. We will enter the intimacy of God, and we will move into His realm. We will speak His language and walk in the direction of the Spirit of God. All of our lives have been transformed. Maybe our family or our friends will not understand it, but it is certain that we carry the anointing of God in us, and with it we can conquer whatever we want.

The Lord carries us from one spiritual success to another greater one, from one level to another. We cannot remain spiritual dwarves, the same as we were the day we got saved, but rather we must grow each day, in the glory of God. But this is only achieved if we enter into intimacy with God, making prayer a way of life.

DEDICATE YOUR MARRIAGE TO GOD'S SERVICE

Claudia, although you and I were the first generation of Christians in our families, we decided from the beginning to rest on the promises of salvation for them. I remember that in a moment of great desperation to see my family saved, the Lord told me, «Son, do not be anxious for them because I have the day and the hour of their salvation.» After that word, I was filled with gratitude towards the Lord because I had his promise, and I never doubted that it would happen.

In reality, all of my family knows the Lord and almost all of my brothers and sisters are in the ministry, but I also enjoy seeing my wife's parents and my brothers-in-law give themselves completely to serving God.

Epilogue

My beloved Claudia

I wanted this book to be the present for our silver wedding anniversary, but I also know that there are many things that are still in our memories because we have shared so many special moments together that we cannot begin to reproduce them all in words even though you and I know them.

For all of that I want to tell you thanks for letting me share my life with you because in these years that we have enjoyed living together we have become united in such a way, one with the other, that we have become fused, and I cannot begin to imagine how my life would be without you.
I think you feel the same way.

I know that these twenty-five years are just the beginning of the best years of blessing that await us. United, you and I, are going to fulfill the purpose of God that He prepared beforehand for us.

Yours in this life and for eternity.

César